THE DIVIDING LINE

Understanding and Applying Biblical Separation

Mark Sidwell

JOURNEYFORTH

Greenville, South Carolina

Library of Congress Cataloging-in-Publication Data
Sidwell, Mark, 1958–
    The dividing line : understanding and applying biblical separation
/ Mark Sidwell
        p. cm.
    Includes bibliographical references and index.
    ISBN 1-57924-074-7
    1. Fundamentalism. 2. Separation from sin—Fundamentalist
churches. 3. Fundamentalist churches—Doctrines. 4. Separation from
sin—Biblical teaching. I. Title.
BT82.2.S53 1998
270.8'2—dc21   98-4767
                                                            CIP

The fact that materials produced by other publishers may be referred
to in this volume does not constitute an endorsement of the content or
theological position of materials produced by such publishers.

All Scripture is quoted from the Authorized King James Version unless
othewise noted.

The Dividing Line: Understanding and Applying Biblical Separation
Mark Sidwell, PhD

Designed by Chris Hartzler
Project editor Don Harrelson

©1998 by BJU Press
Greenville, South Carolina 29614
JourneyForth is a division of BJU Press

ISBN 978-1-57924-074-5

15 14 13 12 11 10 9 8 7 6 5 4 3

Contents

Preface

An unusually large number of books on Fundamentalism written by Fundamentalists have been published since 1990. I personally have had the pleasure of serving as editor for two such books—*"Be Ye Holy": The Call to Christian Separation* by Dr. Fred Moritz and *The Tragedy of Compromise: The Origin and Impact of the New Evangelicalism* by Dr. Ernest Pickering.[1] The question will probably be asked, in light of these and other works, why yet another book on separation?

The purpose of this book is to supplement, not to supplant, other studies. One of my goals is to present an introductory work on the topic that laymen can profitably use. I was surprised how many works on separation assume that readers already know basically what separation is and what terms such as "personal separation" and "ecclesiastical separation" mean. But I do not want to limit this work just to laymen. I hope that pastors, missionaries, Bible teachers, and others involved in Christian ministries may profit as well from its brief discussions.

I also want to help Christians see how separation applies to trends and movements in history and even more in today's religious scene. Perhaps it is my own background in church history, but I have often found my own understanding of biblical teaching deepened as I have seen such teachings worked out and applied in history. I hope, therefore, that the chapters on Fundamentalism, liberalism, Neo-orthodoxy, the New Evangelicalism, the Charismatic movement, and Roman Catholicism will help Christians understand how separation should be applied and practiced.

This book is written from an unashamedly Fundamentalist viewpoint. That fact will be obvious as the reader proceeds. It is not written as a justification of the Fundamentalist position, however, as much as it is a defense of a biblical teaching that Fundamentalists affirm. My goal is to explain and apply the biblical teaching of separation. I wholeheartedly believe that of all contemporary religious movements, Fundamentalism most closely follows the biblical pattern for separation. But I am more concerned that readers practice separation in a biblical manner than I am whether they bear the label "Fundamentalist."

This book is titled *The Dividing Line*. As certainly as Christ separates the sheep from the goats (Matt. 25:32-33), so there is a divide between truth and error. Separation involves discerning that line and taking a stand on the right side of that line. In order to echo Moses' call "Who is on the Lord's side?" (Exod. 32:26), Christians need to know what the sides are and which of the sides is the Lord's. These questions can be answered only through searching the Scripture.

The issues involved in biblical separation are not minor ones. Just before God brought judgment on Korah and his rebellious followers, Moses said to the children of Israel, "Depart, I pray you, from the tents of these wicked men, and touch nothing of theirs, lest ye be consumed in all their sins" (Num. 16:26). Fundamentalists view the dividing line of scriptural separation with that same seriousness.

I recognize that some critics of Fundamentalism view statements such as these as a return to Manichaeism, the ancient dualistic heresy that viewed history as the eternal struggle between spiritual forces of light and darkness.[2] Supposedly, this dualistic point of view causes Christians to be too absolutist in their outlook toward life and toward other people. Also implied in this criticism is that Fundamentalists have too small a view of God. The sovereign God who controls our destinies and comforts our hearts is replaced by a limited deity who needs our aid in a conflict whose outcome is in doubt.

Christians must see the reality of this present spiritual struggle, and it is no favor to anyone—Christian or non-Christian—to pretend that this conflict does not exist. But the fact that this struggle is presently occurring does not mean it is an eternal warfare. One of my former teachers, Edward Panosian, has written, "One who reads the Bible is conscious of a universal struggle between two powers: God and Satan, good and evil, truth and error. This conflict pervades the ages and all the institutions of life, even life itself." But he does not stop there: "While universal, it is not eternal. The Bible assures us that God is Victor, good is triumphant, Truth will be enthroned. This assurance is not only a hoped-for expectation; it is a present reality—not yet realized but no less real."[3]

It is with a view toward that inevitable victory that this book is written.

*   *   *   *

In any published work there is always a need to acknowledge the debts to many people who have helped in its preparation and production. Let me first express my deep gratitude to the Bible faculty of Bob Jones University, whose little pamphlet *Biblical Separation* (1980) laid the basis for Chapters 3-5 of this book. Although the content has been expanded, the basic outline and approach still follow that of the original pamphlet. It helped my confidence in writing those chapters to know that I was drawing on the work of men devoted to both sound biblical scholarship and the pursuit of godliness.

Recognition is also due to Dr. Randy Leedy of the graduate religion faculty at BJU, who did the initial work on this project. His contribution is largest in Chapter 2, and his research on liberalism greatly facilitated the writing of Chapter 7. Likewise, I was guided in the later chapters by Dr. David Beale's syllabus "Fundamentalism and Its Foes: Recent and Current Trends in Religion."

My thanks also goes to Dr. Philip Smith, provost of Bob Jones University, for initiating this project. A special word of gratitude is also due to several others who read all or part of the manuscript: Dr. Bob Jones III, president of BJU; Dr. Thurman Wisdom, dean of the School of Religion; Dr. Dan Olinger of the staff at Bob Jones University Press; and several members of the University's Bible and history faculties: Mr. Richard Gray, Dr. David Beale, Dr. Terry Rude, Dr. Sam Schnaiter, Dr. Randy Jaeggli, Dr. Carl Abrams,

Dr. John Matzko, and Dr. Edward M. Panosian. I appreciate their time and their many valuable suggestions.

And finally, let me say a special word of thanks to my former colleagues at Bob Jones University Press. All I can say is that they have performed at their usual high levels of professionalism, excellence, and Christian dedication. Seeing the results of their labor in print will always remind me how much I owe them and how much I miss working with them.

Defining Our Terms
Chapter 1

Depending on your background, as you pick up this book, the words *biblical separation* may interest you, offend you, or mystify you. Some Christians have grown up in churches with balanced teaching on the idea of separation, and for them it is as much a part of their system of belief as the deity of Christ or the inspiration of the Bible. Others come from situations in which the term seemed to be an excuse for quarrels, antagonism, and hostility. And still others may have been Christians for years and have never heard the term.

Let us say first, then, that the teaching of separation is not just some offbeat idea dreamed up by American Fundamentalists in the twentieth century to justify their practices. Rather, it is a concept clearly taught in the pages of Scripture. That some Christians have not heard of the concept or that others have abused it does not change the fact that separation is a biblical concept to which Christians should give close attention.

What is "biblical separation"? The basic idea is that *Christians should strive to be free from sin.* More specifically, they are to be separated *to* God and *from* sin. There are many ramifications to this idea. You may hear of "personal separation" and "ecclesiastical separation," for example. We will discuss these and other concepts as we go on. But the main point to keep in mind is that Jesus Christ died so that believers would be free from sin. A popular way of summarizing this deliverance is to say that Jesus cleanses sinners from the penalty of sin (the punishment in hell due for their sin), the power of sin (the corrupt habit of sin in the life as a result of natural corruption from Adam), and ultimately the presence of sin (in heaven, where believers will suffer neither inner sinfulness nor association with the sins of others). The practice of separation from sin in this life is one aspect of this deliverance from sin.

Separation and Sanctification

A good place to start in discussing this concept is its location in theology. When you study theology, you find that theologians divide the subject into different headings. *Bibliology* is the doctrine of Scripture. *Christology* is the study of doctrines concerning the person and work of Jesus Christ. Separation fits into this scheme as well. Generally, we look at separation as an expression of sanctification. Sanctification, in turn, is usually discussed as a part of *soteriology,* the doctrines concerning salvation. (*Soteriology* is from the Greek *soteria,* meaning "salvation.")

Soteriology includes a number of topics: biblical teachings such as justification, redemption, propitiation, and adoption. Sanctification is one of these teachings and a very important one. There are two aspects to sanctification, sometimes called "positional" and "progressive" sanctification. When a person is born again by the work of the Holy Spirit and converted, he is "set apart" (which is basically what *sanctify* means). The believer is positionally "in Christ" and therefore set apart to God. The holiness of Christ is credited to the Christian so that God views him as holy (I Cor. 1:30). In this aspect, sanctification is closely connected to justification, in which God declares the sinner righteous by imputing (or crediting) to him the righteousness of Christ.

At the same time, newly converted Christians are far from mature. They will undergo a process of learning more about Christ and about God's Word. Through the power of the Holy Spirit and on the basis of Christ's atonement, believers will by degrees triumph over the power of sin in their lives. In short, believers will, as Peter puts it, "grow in grace, and in the knowledge of our Lord and Saviour Jesus Christ" (II Pet. 3:18). This is "progressive" sanctification. Paul illustrates these two aspects in I Corinthians. He tells the Corinthians, "Ye are sanctified" (6:11). Yet he says earlier, "Ye are yet carnal" (or "fleshly"; 3:3). The Corinthians were sanctified in Christ (positionally), but they had not yet achieved holiness in this life (progressively). Later, Paul beautifully describes progressive sanctification for the Corinthians: "But we all, with open face beholding as in a glass the glory of the Lord, are changed into the same image from glory to glory, even as by the Spirit of the Lord" (II Cor. 3:18).

Look at it this way. When a person is converted, God views him as being as righteous and holy as Jesus Christ because his sin has been covered by the atonement of Christ. In everyday experience, that person is becoming more like Jesus Christ. God sets the goal, and the believer progressively approaches that goal through God's grace. Paul expresses this thought when he says, "Not as though I had already attained, either were already perfect: but I follow after, if that I may apprehend that for which also I am apprehended of Christ Jesus" (Phil. 3:12).

Perhaps you can already see how the idea of separation fits into the doctrine of sanctification. If a Christian is delivered from sin as a result of being "in Christ" and is being progressively delivered from sin in this life, then striving to be separate from sin is only natural. We will look more fully at the theological context of separation in Chapter 2, particularly the important relationship of holiness to separation.

Please keep another thought in mind. The goal of sanctification is "to be conformed to the image" of Jesus Christ (Rom. 8:29), that is, to become more like Christ in thought, action, and all manner of life. Since separation is a part of the doctrine of sanctification, then the goal of separation is to become more like Christ.

We should mention that we can (and will) discuss separation in connection with other doctrines. As we will see, ecclesiology (the doctrine of the church) is an important arena for the practice of separation. Church discipline in particular will take a large place in this discussion. But we do not want to lose our focus on Christlikeness. Even the church, Paul says, is to be sanctified by Christ "that he might present it to himself a glorious church, not having spot, or wrinkle, or any such thing; but that it should be holy and without blemish" (Eph. 5:27).

Aspects of Separation

As we said before, you often hear of what sound like different kinds of separation. Actually, all of these are simply different aspects of the same teaching. Two common terms are *personal* and *ecclesiastical separation.*

Personal separation is the practice of individual sanctification, a refusal to follow the world's philosophy in thought and action. A general supplication in the Church of England's *Book of Common Prayer* contains the plea "From all inordinate and sinful affections; and from all the deceits of the world, the flesh, and the devil, *Good Lord, deliver us.*" Personal separation is the working out of a Christian's deliverance from "the world, the flesh, and the devil" in daily life.

We sometimes think of "worldliness" in terms of certain actions (e.g., drinking, smoking, style of dress). Like any other spiritual problem, however, worldliness begins in the heart. Rolland McCune notes,

> So what is *worldliness?* People often define it in terms of some of its outward activities, but actually it goes much deeper than that. We can define *worldliness* as an affection for and an attachment to some aspect of the present arrangement of things. This attachment includes the world's thought patterns, amusements, fads, habits, philosophies, goals, friendships, practices and lifestyles. Worldliness is a matter of inward attitudes, motives and yearnings as well as outward activities.[1]

Such is Paul's meaning when he tells Christians, "Be not conformed to this world: but be ye transformed by the renewing of your mind" (Rom. 12:2). In Chapter 3 we will look more at how the Scripture addresses this problem of worldliness.

Ecclesiastical separation is in many ways simply an extension of the principles of personal separation. The difference is that it is practiced on the level of an assembly of believers rather than the individual level. The main idea is that Christians refuse to align themselves with false doctrine or unbelief and that they reject the willful practice of disobedience. In the case of theological error,

Christians expose false teachings and warn other Christians against them. In the case of willful disobedience, Christians separate from the disobedient believer to preserve the purity of the church and to restore the erring Christian to full fellowship through discipline. Ecclesiastical separation may involve a church, a group of churches, or even an individual Christian. It might involve a local church leaving a denomination that has become dominated by unbelief or a denomination expelling churches or teachers who hold to false doctrine. It might be as simple as a church disciplining an unrepentant member who has fallen into sin or an individual Christian removing his membership from a church that has departed from the truth.

This form of separation involves not only separation from false teaching but also from unregenerate false teachers, "wolves in sheep's clothing" (Matt. 7:15), who pose as Christians but are actually "false prophets" who teach "damnable heresies" (II Pet. 2:1). Fundamentalists generally consider separation from disobedient Christians a form of ecclesiastical separation, but some others treat this as a separate category.[2]

Some other terms you may hear are *first-degree* and *second-degree separation* (or sometimes *primary* and *secondary separation*). Usually, writers or preachers use these in reference to ecclesiastical separation. First-degree separation is the term for refusing to cooperate with false teachers in religious activities. Second-degree separation is refusing to have fellowship with someone who does not practice first-degree separation. Some writers who use this first- and second-degree distinction argue that although primary separation is good, secondary separation is wrong.[3] Others who use the terminology believe that both are forms of separation that the Christian should practice.[4]

There are problems with this first- and second-degree designation, however. The question of separation is not how close or how far you are to or from a sin. Instead, it is a matter of obeying what the Bible says. If Scripture commands personal separation from the world, separation from false teachers, and separation from Christian brethren who are willfully practicing disobedience, then there are no "degrees" about it. "Separation does not really admit of degrees: It is directed to the other person because of *his* deviation from Scripture in whatever ways he may express them. If he runs with the wrong crowd, separation at this point is from *him* and not from the crowd he runs with."[5]

Two other terms you sometimes hear in connection with separation are *inclusivism* and *exclusivism.* Simply put, exclusivism is the separatist position, and inclusivism is the nonseparatist position. The Fundamentalist-Modernist controversy of the 1920s illustrates these terms. The Fundamentalists sought to exclude liberals from their denominations—their churches, schools, mission boards, and other agencies. The Modernists (the liberal party), however, did not seek to exclude the Fundamentalists. Rather, they wanted to include all shades of belief within the denominations, everything from Fundamentalism to outright liberalism. For the separatist, the exclusion of false teaching is necessary, and the inclusion of such teaching in a religious fellowship is a violation of God's Word.

We could mention other issues under this topic of separation. Some see the idea of separation of church and state as another expression of biblical separation.[6] This is certainly an idea worth considering. In this book, however, we will focus on three issues in separation: separation from the world, separation from false teachers, and separation from disobedient brethren. We will not exhaust the topic of separation, but we will at least introduce you to the main concepts and their biblical bases.

Separation in History

If you were to read (or have already read) discussions of biblical separation, you would note that many of the recorded controversies over separation seem to center in American churches in the twentieth century. This fact might cause some to conclude that separation is some new idea dreamed up by American Fundamentalists. The idea of separation, however, has a long history.

We should note, however, that history is not the test of truth. We do not judge the rightness of separation by whether it has historical precedent but whether it accords with the Bible. None-theless, the historical precedent for separation helps us understand the nature of separation and gives us some idea of how it is practiced.

Personal Separation in History

Throughout history, the idea of personal separation from world-liness has not been much questioned, although there have been lively debates about what constitutes "worldliness." Such separa-tion has long been considered one of the marks of a Christian. In the second century, the anonymous *Epistle to Diognetus* describes in what way Christians are "distinguished from the rest of man-kind." Among other qualities, the author says, "Every foreign country is a fatherland to them, and every fatherland is foreign. They marry like all other men and they beget children; but they do not cast away their offspring. They have their meals in common, but not their wives. They find themselves in the flesh, and yet they live not after the flesh. Their existence is on earth, but their citizenship is in heaven."[7]

In the third century, Tertullian of North Africa warned against the bloodshed and pervasive immorality of Roman "spectacles" (athletic games and theaters). "What concord can the Holy Spirit have with spectacles?" he asks.[8] Tertullian argues, "For what sort of conduct is it to go from the assembly of God to the assembly of the devil? from sky to stye, as the proverb has it? those hands you have uplifted to God, to tire them out clapping an actor? with those lips, with which you have uttered *Amen* . . . to cheer for a gladiator?"[9]

The practice of monasticism as found in Roman Catholic and Eastern churches is actually an exaggeration of the principle of separation. In response to the growing worldliness of the church, some Christians began to live apart as hermits or in monastic communities. The monks sought to be separate from the corruption of the world and devote themselves to service for God. They were right in their desire to be free from worldly corruption. Unfortu-nately, in their zeal they identified isolation with separation. Paul warns the Corinthians that they could not avoid contact with unregenerate sinners, "for then must ye needs go out of the world" (I Cor. 5:10; see also John 17:15). Monks also tended to see the discipline of monasticism as a means to greater holiness. The Scripture rather presents discipline as the outgrowth of the work of God's grace in the Christian's heart.

We usually associate the Puritans and the Separatists (such as the Pilgrims of Plymouth Colony) of England and New England with ecclesiastical separation. These believers sought either the cleansing of the Church of England or outright separation from it. But alongside that desire for a pure church was a desire for pure lives. The word *Puritan* is sometimes used as an insult for someone who has strict moral standards. These critics are simply caricaturing the desire for holiness that characterized the Puritans. The Pilgrims, in fact, came to New England partly because they were concerned about the worldly lifestyles that their children were learning in the Netherlands.

A more modern example of the stress on personal separation is the Holiness movement that arose within Methodism in the 1800s. Those familiar with Holiness Christians often identify them by their strict standards of behavior. Some of the most conservative, for example, oppose the wearing of any jewelry, even wedding bands. Others hold that Christians should not own television sets because of the worldly influences they introduce into the home. (This view is seeming less extreme as television programming continues to degenerate.) These outward practices are but visible expressions of the Holiness Christians' desire to separate from the world and be conformed to Christ. They ask, as their founder and inspiration John Wesley asked, "Who is he that will open his mouth against being cleansed from all pollution, both of flesh and spirit; or against having all the mind that was in Christ, and walking in all things as Christ walked?"[10]

Ecclesiastical Separation in History

Ecclesiastical separation is likewise no new idea, although the practice has varied through the centuries. Often such separation was practiced through church discipline in expelling false teachers or flagrantly immoral members. In the second century, the church at Rome was much impressed with the charm and eloquence of a teacher named Marcion. But then they found out he was teaching that the God of the Old Testament was evil whereas the God of the New Testament was good and that only certain books of the Bible (mostly Paul's epistles and an abridged version of the Gospel of Luke) were inspired. The church expelled him for teaching these heresies.

Likewise in the fourth century, the Councils of Nicea (325) and Constantinople (381) condemned the teaching of Arius, who believed that Christ was not God but only a great created being (a teaching similar to that of the Jehovah's Witnesses today). The church excluded the Arians for their error. In fact, as Rousas Rushdoony points out, the early church councils were not designed to promote unity at all costs, as is commonly thought, but to draw clearly the line between truth and error.[11]

Another example of ecclesiastical separation is the departing of various protest groups from the institutional church before the Reformation. The Donatists, for instance, arose in the fourth century to protest lax church discipline. They particularly insisted that people who had denied their faith under persecution could never be readmitted to the church. Eventually, the Donatists set up their own church with its own buildings, sacraments, and hierarchy of bishops.

Several groups also separated from the institutional church in the Middle Ages. The Waldenses (dating from the eleventh century) were persecuted for their desire to translate and preach the Word of God without ordination, for their rejection of immoral priests, and for other teachings. Most other separatist medieval groups, however, were heretical on some major points of doctrine, and they do not always provide the best model of separatism.[12]

The Reformation is one of the clearest examples of ecclesiastical separation. Protestant reformers such as Martin Luther, John Calvin, Ulrich Zwingli, and John Knox opposed the false teachings that had grown up in the Roman Catholic Church. The reformers insisted that Christians are bound only by the authority of Scripture (not Scripture *and* church tradition) and are justified by faith alone (not faith *and* good works). These and other teachings caused the reformers to separate from Rome and form their own churches. The Anabaptists, one of the Protestant groups, even went so far as to advocate an early form of the separation of church and state.

As we mentioned before, some of the great battles over separation were fought in the United States in the twentieth century. We will look at these briefly in Chapter 6. However, one of the best modern examples of ecclesiastical separation occurred in Great Britain in the 1800s. English Baptist Charles H. Spurgeon became concerned about the "downgrade" of biblical teaching within the Baptist Union, a major fellowship of British Baptists to which Spurgeon belonged. Spurgeon warned that liberals were undercutting teachings such as the Bible's inspiration. Finally, Spurgeon himself left the Baptist Union. He wrote, "The bounden duty of a true believer towards men who profess to be Christians, and yet deny the Word of the Lord, and reject the fundamentals of the gospel, is to come out from among them."[13]

Conclusion

The chapters that follow will develop and illustrate the idea of biblical separation. We will see how the Scriptures teach this important principle. As you read these pages, however, do not lose sight of the basic idea: *Christians should strive to be free from sin.* As Rolland McCune notes, the apostle Paul summarizes the basic idea of separation when he writes, "Abhor that which is evil; cleave to that which is good" (Rom. 12:9).[14]

Separation in Theological Context
Chapter 2

It may have occurred to you in the last chapter that if separation is simply striving to be free from sin, why would any Christian question the practice? Virtually no professing believer is going to argue that a Christian should not seek to be free from sin. For a "Christian" objection to separation to be credible, it needs at least to appear to have a biblical basis. One tactic is to argue about the details in Bible passages that separatists cite. The nonseparatist will attempt to prove that such passages do not actually teach separation, at least as the separatists practice it. We will deal with this criticism in Chapters 3-5, where we discuss the biblical basis for separation.

Another common tactic used to argue against separation is to set it against another biblical teaching. Opponents of separation, in other words, formulate dichotomies. A dichotomy is a statement of two mutually exclusive ideas. The cliché "You can't have your cake and eat it too" is a dichotomy. Quite literally, you cannot eat a piece of cake and at the same time save it for later. The problem, as we will see, is that the arguments being used are false dichotomies.[1] Opponents of separation are setting biblical ideas in opposition to separation that do not really exclude separation.

Those who argue by dichotomies nonetheless have a point. One of the dangers in arguing an important point of doctrine and practice is the possibility of imbalance. We all recognize the need for balance in many areas of life. A long-distance runner strives for an optimum balance between speed and energy conservation. If he errs too far in either direction, he will finish poorly—if at all. A dietician may tout the nutritional value of certain foods, but she would never recommend a diet consisting of just one such food. Foods that are highly beneficial in proper proportion can do great damage if consumed in excessive quantities. Students of Scripture must like-wise develop a keen sense of balance. Theology deals with many issues that cannot be reduced to a single fact that is demonstrably true and whose opposite is demonstrably false. Instead, these issues involve seemingly opposing pairs of truths that the Christian must hold in proper balance.

Some issues in life are simple. A mathematician knows that $2 \times 3 = 6$ is true and that $2 \times 3 \neq 6$ is false. But consider a theological proposition: God is one. This statement is consistent with biblical teaching and is therefore true. However, the opposite, that God is more than one (Father, Son, and Holy Spirit), is also true in a sense. (To be more precise, we should say, "God is in three.") Theologians must constantly balance truths that operate in tension with one another. (Remember, by the way, that *everyone* is a theologian at least informally, since everyone believes *something* about God.) Just like the runner who must constantly balance speed and endurance in setting his pace, theologians must pay attention to contrasting biblical emphases. They must formulate their understanding of truth in a way that adequately accounts for both. In the case of the oneness of God, a careful study of Scripture uncovers the doctrine of the Trinity: God is a single essence comprising three persons.

What teachings do critics offer to offset separation? Christian unity is an obvious one. The Bible's warnings against the sin of schism are another. Likewise the Scriptures' commands for association with others (for evangelism and witness) present an apparent contrast to separation. We will look at each of these dichotomies. The most important dichotomy involving separation is the alleged tension between holiness and love. We will devote the largest portion of this chapter to that topic.

Christian Unity vs. Separation

The Bible unquestionably issues a call to Christian unity in tension with the call to separation. "Behold," says David, "how good and how pleasant it is for brethren to dwell together in unity!" (Ps. 133:1). John 17:20-23, where Jesus prays "that they all may be one," and Ephesians 4:1-16, where Paul tells believers "to keep the unity of the Spirit in the bond of peace," are two of the major passages that reflect God's desire for His people to maintain spiritual unity. In the 1950s and 1960s, when he was confronted with the call for uniting churches in Great Britain at the expense of truth, Bible expositor D. Martyn Lloyd-Jones carefully reviewed these two passages. He concluded that neither passage supported the idea of unity apart from the truth.[2]

Lloyd-Jones points out that in John 17 the unity Christ prays for is restricted to believers, "them which thou hast given me." Lloyd-Jones notes that "we must emphasize the element of separation and distinction. Our Lord does not pray for the world; He prays only for these people who have been given to Him."[3] Second, Lloyd-Jones says the origin of unity is in the work of God. Christians *maintain* the unity God has given and do not *create* unity. "Our Lord is not dealing with something at which we should aim. . . . It is a prayer to God to keep the unity that He, through His preaching, has already brought into existence among these people."[4] Third, he says the unity commanded in John 17 must be of the same nature as the unity between the Father and the Son: "that they may be one, even as we are one." Only those regenerated by the Holy Spirit and brought into union with the Father through Christ can enjoy this kind of unity.

In dealing with Ephesians 4, Lloyd-Jones points out that Ephesians 1-3 shows that this passage relates to those who are already "in Christ," who are already saved. He mentions that again the idea is to maintain, not create, unity because unity is "of the Spirit"—created by the Holy Spirit. In both John 17 and Ephesians 4, Lloyd-Jones says, "the question of unity must never be put first. We must never start with it, but always remember the order stated so clearly in Acts 2:42, where fellowship follows doctrine: 'They continued stedfastly in the apostles' doctrine and fellowship, and in breaking of bread, and in prayers.' "[5]

Objections based on the Bible's teaching on unity among brethren are then fairly easy for the separatist to answer. The Bible clearly teaches that any genuine spiritual unity assumes a common commitment to God and to His truth. Jesus prayed that believers would be one as He and His Father are one, and They do not disagree on the fundamentals! Where there is no real Christian unity, there cannot possibly be any sin in separation. By no means may Fundamentalists ignore God's commands for unity. However, "the starting point in considering the question of unity must always be regeneration and belief of the truth."[6]

Schism vs. Separation

Another danger the Christian must balance against separation is the sin of schism. Lloyd-Jones defines schism as "division in the true visible church about matters that are not sufficient to justify division or separation."[7] Many times the Bible warns against schisms (divisions) in the church. (See I Cor. 12:25; Rom. 16:17; Gal. 5:20.) We use the word *heresy* to describe a dangerously false teaching, but in Scripture the word often has the meaning of "division" (I Cor. 11:19; Gal. 5:20). *Heresy* came to mean "false doctrine" probably because false teachings create divisions.

The fullest teaching against schism is found in I Corinthians. The apostle Paul urges the Corinthian believers "that ye all speak the same thing, and that there be no divisions among you; but that ye be perfectly joined together in the same mind and in the same judgment" (1:10). He reports how he has heard that they are divided into factions in which they are saying, "I am of Paul; and I of Apollos; and I of Cephas; and I of Christ" (v. 12). "Is Christ divided?" he asks. "Was Paul crucified for you?" (v. 13). Later Paul firmly condemns these divisions, saying that they are desecrating their celebration of the Lord's Supper (11:17-22). The church is a body, he says, and there should be no divisions within the body (12:12-25, especially v. 25).

Schism is clearly a sin. But is separation the same thing as schism? We should note that schism can exist without separation. Lloyd-Jones points out that the Corinthian church suffered from schism, but it had not actually broken into separate groups.[8] More important, as we will see in the following chapters, God commands separation in certain circumstances. Obeying God's commands out of a pure heart can never be a sin, and God's Word does not contradict itself. "Any separation which is made in obedience to the clear command of Scripture (because of opposition to false doctrine or some other serious error) cannot possibly be the sin of schism."[9] As in the case of Christian unity, we cannot just dismiss a major biblical teaching to accommodate separation. But likewise we cannot dismiss separation out of an uncalled-for fear of schism.[10]

Association vs. Separation

A third argument is an appeal to the clear biblical command to associate even with sinners in order to witness to them of salvation through Christ. L. Nelson Bell criticizes separatism, saying that "the 'doctrine of separation' can lead people to abandon the opportunity for witness where it is most greatly needed. The Bible teaches that we should be separated from sin, but not from the sinner."[11] How valid is such a charge?

Real unity between Christians and unbelievers cannot exist, but, truly, even our separation from unbelievers cannot be absolute, for, as Paul says, "then must ye needs go out of the world" (I Cor. 5:10). A believer's total isolation from the world is not only impossible but also undesirable. Jesus has left us "in the world" (John 17:11) in order that He might send us "into the world" (John 17:18). Furthermore, the sinless Son of God Himself is our example of living within a sinful world. The verse just cited, along with eight other verses in John, refer to Jesus' having been sent into the world.[12] The only way God can save sinners is to come into contact with them, and if God Himself does so, His servants must do the same. There is indeed a necessary association of the saved with the unsaved.

We will make a fatal mistake, however, if we think that our necessary association with people who are not right with God justifies our patterning ourselves after them and sharing their sinful lifestyles. With Jesus as our pattern, we can be certain that it is God's will for us while we are "in the world" (John 17:11) not to be "of the world" (John 17:14, 16). Just as Jesus lived and moved among sinners, in order to minister to them, without ever sinning Himself, so believers must aim to remain free from any taint of evil as they serve God among the ungodly. Jesus prayed for us to this end: "I pray not that thou shouldest take them out of the world, but that thou shouldest keep them from the evil" (John 17:15). Jude tells us, "And others save with fear, pulling them out of the fire," but warns that, while doing so, we must hate "even the garment spotted by the flesh" (Jude 23).[13]

So we do find in Scripture a pair of requirements in tension with one another: the requirement to separate ourselves from evil and the opposing requirement to associate ourselves with evil people. Believers who seriously pursue these two requirements, though, must not expect evil people to understand or appreciate their posture toward them. Jesus says, "The world hath hated them, because they are not of the world, even as I am not of the world" (John 17:14). The world that crucified Jesus opposes His people in every age for the same reason that they killed Him. It is not surprising, then, to find the world objecting to separatist practice.

Holiness vs. Love

The nonseparatist tends to see love as so transcending other teachings of Scripture that it modifies commands to separate. There is no denying the fact that Jesus identifies love for God and neighbor as the first and greatest commandment (Matt. 22:36-40) and that the apostles reinforce this assessment (Rom. 13:9; Gal. 5:14; James 2:8). The nonseparatist concludes that separation as Fundamentalists practice it is a violation of love and is therefore unbiblical. Ronald Nash, for example, charges Fundamentalism with "sectarianism, separatism and total ignoring of the law of love."[14]

The separatist, on the other hand, finds his firmest ground in the Bible's pervasive emphasis on holiness. He separates from evil because God is separate from evil and because He calls His people to imitate Him on that point: "Be ye holy; for I am holy" (I Pet. 1:16, quoting Lev. 20:7). Fred Moritz rightly titled his study of separation *"Be Ye Holy": The Call to Christian Separation*, observing, "The purpose of separation is the ongoing effort by the local church or the believer to imitate the holiness of God."[15] The

Fundamentalist concludes that love as nonseparatists practice it is a violation of holiness and is therefore unbiblical.

Have we found here another point of tension? Do holiness and love "moderate" one another so that we do not go to an extreme in either direction? In other words, does love require us to be less holy than we might like and holiness require us to be less loving than we might like? This is how it works in the case of the long-distance runner's tension between speed and energy conservation. In that case the ideal in one direction must be moderated in light of a balancing consideration in the opposite direction.

Holiness and love, however, are not opposites like some of the pairs we have discussed earlier. The fact that some people view the two as opposites does not mean that they *are* opposites. We should start with a clear understanding of the key terms involved: *holiness* and *love*. Once we understand these terms, we will see that many nonseparatists are reacting to a misconception about holiness, while some separatists react to a misconception about love. These misconceptions often arise from unbiblical practices carried out under the guise of holiness or of love. If separatists misunderstand holiness, they will practice separation in unbiblical ways that call for rebuke. And the same holds true for the nonseparatist's misunderstanding of love.[16]

The Meaning of Holiness

Holiness is essentially uniqueness or "differentness." It does not follow, of course, that just any kind of uniqueness is commendable. A lunatic is noticeably different from other people, but that difference is not commendable. The point of difference with which biblical holiness concerns itself is that around which the whole creation revolves: the difference between good and evil, between moral light and darkness, between God and Satan. Our fallen world is characterized by evil, darkness, and the domination of Satan. To be holy in the biblical sense is to manifest a character displaying goodness, light, and the rule of God.

The Bible expresses this uniqueness as moral purity and separation from that which is unclean. It is on this basis that Ernest

Pickering writes, "God is a separatist. He is separated from all that is evil. Holiness is a principle of His nature. It is consistent, therefore, to expect that bodies which He would establish upon this earth to represent Him would be required to be holy (separated) as well. They would be expected to mirror His character."[17]

As we noted in Chapter 1, through justification God regards the believer as being as righteous and holy as Jesus is. The goal of progressive sanctification is to grow toward greater holiness and purity of life. Critics of Fundamentalism do not deride holiness or purity as such. Rather they imply that there is something false or artificial about the Fundamentalist stress on holiness. One writer typifies this criticism when he characterizes Fundamentalism as pursuing a "prideful quest for purity."[18] Often, Fundamentalism is caricatured as an overemphasis on externals as expressions of holiness.

But one implication of the biblical teaching of holiness—perhaps the most important one—is that holiness is not primarily an external attribute. Satan's external appearance, the Bible says, can be indistinguishable from that of God's angels (II Cor. 11:14). The fact that he looks good does not mean that he is good. The same is true of people. Jesus describes the scribes and Pharisees as white-washed tombs—outwardly beautiful but utterly corrupt within (Matt. 23:27-28). Holiness is first and foremost a matter of the heart. God gave Israel the physical rite of circumcision as a sign of this nation's "differentness" from its neighbors. But the circumcision He really wanted to see was the circumcision of the people's hearts. This topic is mentioned seven times in the Old Testament (Lev. 26:41; Deut. 10:16; 30:6; Jer. 4:4; 9:25-26; Ezek. 44:7, 9), and Paul drives it home in Romans 2:29—"Circumcision is that of the heart, in the spirit, and not in the letter; whose praise is not of men, but of God."

If the character of the world were morally neutral, you could argue that believers may be like the world without compromising the holiness of their hearts. Remember, the point of difference with which true holiness concerns itself is the difference between right and wrong. Where right and wrong are not at stake, holiness demands no difference. Whether to wear a red or a blue shirt is not an issue of holiness unless it becomes a question of right and wrong when, for example, a parent instructs a child to wear one or the other. But the character of the world is not morally neutral. The world's entertainment, for example, reflects the ungodliness of a worldly heart. A Christian whose consumption of entertainment is indistinguishable from the world's has no right to claim that his heart is truly holy toward God. Wherever there is a choice to be made between what reflects the character of God and what reflects the character of Satan, the heart that chooses for God is the holy heart, and the heart that sides with Satan is unholy. Since true holiness is that of the heart, it follows that those who conform to the world's pattern on moral issues are unholy people. Jesus' teaching supports this claim, for He states that immorality proceeds from within, out of the heart (Mark 7:14-23).

A truly holy life, then, is one that is different from the world in a way that identifies it with God. Holiness begins in the heart; without holiness of heart there can be no holiness of life. But holiness never ends in the heart. The disposition of the heart manifests itself outwardly, to an increasing degree as a believer matures in Christ.

So what are the differences of life that identify a holy person with God? Consider an illustration from the life of Frederick Douglass (1818-95), a slave who later escaped bondage and became a leading opponent of slavery and defender of the rights of black Americans. As a boy, while still a slave, Douglass had heard the gospel with interest. He was happy at the age of fifteen when his master, Thomas Auld, professed conversion during a Methodist revival meeting. Auld testified proudly of his conversion, and he often invited ministers to come visit with him. Yet Frederick saw no difference in Auld's treatment of his slaves. When Douglass began attending a black Sunday school led by a free black, a mob from the Methodist church, led by Auld himself, broke up the meeting with violence. Douglass was later sent to another master, Edward Covey, who also claimed to be a devout Methodist. But Covey was a "slave breaker" whose job it was to break the wills of stubborn slaves. He beat Douglass often, on one occasion until the slave was bloody. Douglass observed these men, saw even Methodist preachers using the whip on slaves, and finally concluded that "of all slave holders . . . religious ones are the worst. I have found them, almost invariably, the vilest, meanest, and basest of their class."[19] Disgusted with such men, Douglass turned his back on evangelical Christianity.

Consider another illustration. J. Frank Norris (1877-1952) was a fiery Fundamentalist known as "the Texas tornado." He denounced liberalism in the Southern Baptist Convention so pointedly that the convention expelled him. His paper, with more than eighty thousand subscribers, printed scathing attacks on evolution, Communism, and especially religious liberalism. Norris was unquestionably a powerful preacher who built large churches in Fort Worth, Texas, and Detroit, Michigan—and pastored them both at the same time. His radio broadcasts covered most of the nation. He became perhaps the best-known Fundamentalist in the South.

But at the same time, Norris was notoriously difficult to get along with. Evangelist John R. Rice broke a nine-year association with Norris because he felt Norris was trying to control him. Norris called the evangelist a heretic and warned Rice that he would never get anywhere without Norris's support. Rice even briefly stopped calling himself a "Fundamentalist" because the term was so associated with Norris.[20] When G. B. Vick and a number of other men broke from Norris to form the Baptist Bible Fellowship in 1950, Norris savaged them in print. He called them "gangsters" and charged them and their families with adultery, sodomy, and other moral offenses. Norris's own son left his father's church and founded another church in Fort Worth. The angry father offered to pay for the younger Norris to change his last name.[21] Probably the most infamous event in Norris's life took place in 1926. In the middle of a prolonged controversy with the Catholic mayor of Fort Worth, Norris shot and killed a supporter of the mayor in the pastor's study. Norris said that he thought his life was being threatened, and a jury acquitted him of murder. But the incident forever branded him as a "gun-totin' parson."

Of course, the hypocrisy of professing Christians could not excuse Frederick Douglass before God. And God was able to use even a man as flawed as J. Frank Norris to defend His truth. But holiness does not consist in professing conversion and attending church or even defending the Christian faith. These are, at most, the outward signs of a holy heart. The differences that identify a person with God are supernatural character traits such as selflessness toward others, joy in the midst of suffering, a genuine love of the Scriptures, and a prayerful recognition of and confidence in God's hand at work where others see only fate and random chance. A minister may certainly defend the Faith and be characterized by holiness, but he will conduct his ministry as the outgrowth of a genuinely holy heart. A sincere concern for God and man softens a Christian's manners and seasons his speech.

You see, someone who claims to live carefully by biblical standards of holiness can be just like the Pharisees, whose circumcision affected their flesh but not their heart. To live just like the Pharisees is, at least partly, to lack love for God and for your neighbor. Onlookers who observe such pharisaical lives are correct to point out the obvious lack of love. It does not follow, however, that holiness is less important than love. The onlooker is reacting against a false holiness rather than against true holiness. He is reacting to a hypocritical stress on externals and not a difference in lifestyle that clearly reflects the character of God in contrast to that of the world.

Do not suppose, though, that true holiness is always clearly understood and appreciated. Since the world has always hated God, it will always hate those who are like Him. But it is one thing to be hated for manifesting the character of God that is such a rebuke to sinners. It is quite another to be disdained as a hypocrite who pretends to be holy while in fact living the same kind of sinful life as his worldly neighbors.

The Meaning of Love

Just as holiness is often misperceived as a fastidious preoccupation with external details to the neglect of inner character, love is often misperceived as a feeling of goodwill and an unconditionally affirmative attitude toward all people as they are. The loving thing to do in any situation, this misunderstanding assumes, is the thing that makes people feel accepted and increases their self-esteem.

The Bible leaves no doubt, though, about what genuine love is. Since the Bible teaches that God is the source of love (I John 4:16, 19), we must form our conception of love on the basis of how the Bible describes God's love. Perhaps the best place to begin is the most familiar verse in the Bible: "For God so loved the world, that he gave his only begotten Son, that whosoever believeth in him should not perish, but have everlasting life" (John 3:16). God's love is something that prompted Him to sacrifice Himself for the benefit of those He loves. Love is not a feeling of attachment, for elsewhere the Bible teaches clearly that sinners are revolting to God and that He is full of wrath toward them. Paul reinforces the self-sacrificial character of God's love: "But God commendeth his love toward us, in that, while we were yet sinners, Christ died for us" (Rom. 5:8).

So let us lay down a provisional definition of love along these lines: love is a disposition to act in the highest interests of the loved one, regardless of the cost to the one who loves. Such a disposition may or may not involve an emotional attachment to the loved object. Emotion is a negotiable component; self-sacrificial commitment is not. A love that lacks this commitment is a kind of love other than that which God exercises and commands us to exercise.

Now the question arises whether God really commands us to have this kind of love, or whether this is a love that only He can have, a love far above human capacity. In the first place, the New Testament's commands to love invariably use the same word for love that normally describes God's love, even though several synonyms were available. This is not a conclusive argument, though. The same word is also used for lesser kinds of love (e.g., Matt. 23:6; John 12:43), and the Bible sometimes uses the synonyms to describe God's love (John 5:20; 16:27).

The passage in which Jesus commands us to love our enemies comes very close to requiring a self-sacrificial love like God's (Matt. 5:43-48). And in John's Gospel the requirement to love as God loves becomes crystal clear. "As the Father hath loved me, so have I loved you: continue ye in my love," Jesus says (John 15:9). But does this mean to continue loving as Christ loves or to continue being an object of Christ's love? The passage continues: "If ye keep my commandments, ye shall abide in my love; even as I have kept my Father's commandments, and abide in his love" (v. 10). So it does not sound as though Jesus is commanding the disciples to exercise love but is rather commanding them to live so that they may continue to be objects of His love. But the passage is not finished. What commandment(s) must they keep? "This is my commandment, That ye love one another, *as I have loved you*" (v. 12; emphasis added). Still, Jesus has not explicitly demanded self-sacrifice. Perhaps He means that it should be true that we love one another just as it is true that He loved us, not necessarily that we should love one another just as much as He loved us. But, again, read on: "Greater love hath no man than this, that a man lay down his life for his friends" (v. 13). There is no avoiding the fact that the Bible requires believers to love with the same kind of love as that with which God loves them.

John learned Jesus' teaching about love. Decades later he described love as one of the preeminent qualities of the Christian life (I John 3:10-23). He wrote, "My little children, let us not love in word, neither in tongue; but in deed and in truth" (v. 18). John stresses that believers love one another with a divine kind of self-sacrificial love. The presence or absence of this sort of love is directly related to our assurance of salvation (v. 19), and John gives love an importance equal with that of faith in Christ (v. 23).

The Bible clearly lays upon believers a demand to love as God loves. Although it is impossible to love to the full extent that God loves, it is nevertheless possible, through the work of the indwelling Holy Spirit, to love with the same kind of love as God has, a self-sacrificing commitment to serve the highest interests of those we love. We see this in Scripture in the example of Paul, who wrote to the Corinthians (his most troublesome church, by the way), "And I will very gladly spend and be spent for you; though the more abundantly I love you, the less I be loved" (II Cor. 12:15). Paul follows the pattern of divine love. So should every Christian.

The Relationship Between Holiness and Love

Remember that we are exploring whether holiness and love are opposites that we must balance against each other as we formulate our principles of separation. We have defined our terms: holiness is a difference from the world that identifies us with God in opposition to Satan, and love is a self-sacrificing commitment to act in the highest interest of those we love. Once we understand these terms, we can see that there is no reason to limit either of them. Is there a degree of Godlike holiness beyond which it is harmful to go? Can we be too much like God and too little like the world? Regarding love, can we be so willing to sacrifice for the sake of others that we displease God or harm someone? Obviously, there is no limitation to be placed upon these virtues of holiness and love, and we will spend our Christian lives continually growing in our exercise of them. In fact, we really can equate them with sinlessness. To the extent that we are like God, we do not sin. To the extent that we strive unselfishly to press forward the work of God in people's lives, we do not sin. If holiness and love, properly understood, equate with sinlessness, then we can see that we must place no limit on either.

Nonseparatists, then, who complain, "You Fundamentalists would do better to quit worrying about holiness and get concerned about love" set up a false tension between these two virtues. Fundamentalists would make a mistake if they respond by reversing the terms: "You compromisers should quit worrying so much about love and get concerned about holiness." That response accepts the premise that those two virtues are in tension. Worse for Fundamentalists, nonseparatists have the Bible on their side when they rank love before holiness, since Jesus Himself singles out love rather than holiness as the first and greatest commandment.

We must hasten to add, however, that it does not follow that holiness is unimportant. In rebuking the Pharisees, Jesus put these virtues in order like this: "But woe unto you, Pharisees! for ye tithe mint and rue and all manner of herbs, and pass over [i.e., overlook] judgment [i.e., justice] and the love of God: these ought ye to have done, and not to leave the other undone" (Luke 11:42). The error of the Pharisees is that they attempted to be holy without having laid a foundation of love for God on which to build that holiness. A holiness not based on genuine love for God will always be a false holiness. The command to imitate God's holiness presupposes a love for God. Without that love there is no motive for obeying that command. If today's Fundamentalists try to be holy without a genuine love for God and man in their hearts, they will become modern-day Pharisees deserving the rebuke of those who see through their hypocrisy.

But there is a better way. Once the foundation of true love for God and neighbor is laid in the heart, a person's reason for living is to serve God and man rather than himself. And this order is crucial. Jesus ranks love for God as the first commandment because a love for man that does not keep God's interests as the highest priority will always go astray and content itself with serving man's baser interests. Notice these words: "By this we know that we love the children of God, when we love God, and keep his commandments" (I John 5:2). You see, love for God must come first, and love for man inevitably follows, just as love in general must come first, and holiness follows.[22]

Here is the point, then, at which we have been driving. Those who truly love will zealously pursue true holiness, since people's likeness to Christ is both God's interest and their own highest interest. The proper response of the Fundamentalist who is charged with a lack of love, then, is twofold. First, he must examine himself and consider the validity of the charges, repenting of any failure that may validate them. Second, having reaffirmed his conviction that he acts in obedience to Scripture, for the sake of God and man rather than himself, he should point out any evident misunderstanding by the nonseparatist of the true meaning of love and holiness.

Then he should commit himself ever more fully to the biblical path of holiness prompted by love.

Conclusion

The theological context of separation demands of us two things. First, it demands that we balance Scripture's requirement of separation against its requirements of unity and association and its warnings against schism. As they practice separation, Fundamentalists must take God's desires concerning Christian unity seriously. They must guard against the sin of schism, which separation could easily become if not practiced scripturally. They must realize the necessity of association with sinners for evangelism and witness. Otherwise biblical separation becomes unscriptural isolation.

Second, the theological context demands that we recognize that a scripturally balanced separation is an expression both of holiness and of love. We must simultaneously maximize these two character traits of God in our daily living, not balance one against the other. We will fail in the areas of both holiness and love if we become excessive either in separatism or in inclusivism. Of course, we must define "excessive" in light of what the Bible teaches, not in light of what makes us comfortable. To develop and apply that scriptural definition will be the task of the remainder of this book.

Separation from the World
Chapter 3

In the first two chapters, we discussed broad but vital issues concerning separation. We have argued that biblical separation is a practice rooted in the teaching of Scripture. It is time now to look closely at the specific scriptural evidence for this doctrine. The Bible alone is our authority for doctrine and practice (II Tim. 3:16-17). The Scripture does not merely inform us of God's will; it also guides us in how we should live and act (Ps. 119:105; Prov. 6:23). It is attention to Scripture, guided by the Holy Spirit, that will enable us to maintain a balanced view of separation. We need to avoid the extremes of ignoring the principle of separation entirely or separating unnecessarily over minor points of interpretation and custom.

We will discuss separation under three divisions: separation from the world (this chapter), separation from false teachers (Chapter 4), and separation from disobedient brethren (Chapter 5). Our goal is to demonstrate that separation is not optional but absolutely necessary when circumstances demand it. It is simply a matter of obeying the Word of God. Furthermore, there are spiritual benefits to separation, such as fellowship with God. Because the Bible contains many Old Testament examples as well as New Testament warnings and commands concerning separation, we will also cite Old Testament parallels to the New Testament teaching. Separation, we will see, is not an obscure teaching dragged out of some forgotten corner. It runs through the whole of God's Word.

It is always good to know our limitations, though. Three chapters in a slender book such as this cannot exhaustively cover all the biblical teaching concerning separation. We will touch on the major points and note the main evidence, but you will need to continue meditating on this concept as you read God's Word and hear it preached. Also, it is important to keep in mind that categories such as personal and ecclesiastical separation often overlap. False teaching occurs in the world as well as in the church. Sinful practices of the unsaved sometimes enter the church. These classifications are guides to help us understand God's Word, but Scripture does not always fit neatly into manmade categories.

Finally, although we will attempt to be clear and specific, it is impossible to lay down absolute rules to prescribe the proper course of action for every situation that may arise in the life and ministry of a Christian. No mature Christian can escape the responsibility of making his own decisions. When some specific situation arises, you must follow principle to determine your response. We want to help you make certain that your decisions or actions do not violate clear biblical teachings and that your principles are in harmony with the Scripture's teaching.

With these thoughts in mind, let us look more closely at the first of our topics: separation from the world.

Definitions

In this chapter and the two that follow, we will introduce the discussion with definitions of basic terms. These will help you follow the arguments of a particular passage by showing you how these terms are used in the whole of Scripture.

World System: By "world system" we mean the unregenerate people of this earth as organized and dominated by Satan, "the god of this world" (literally, this *age*). This system opposes Christ and His goals for the earth (John 15:18-19). Sometimes we call the world system simply "the world," but it is very important that we do not confuse the physical world with the spiritually corrupt realm of Satan. The physical world was created by God and is sustained by Him (Gen. 1:1; Col. 1:16-17). Although it suffers from the effects of sin (Rom. 8:19-22), it is still the possession of God. The world system, on the other hand, is the realm of Satan characterized by rebellion against God.

Worldliness: We sometimes talk about worldliness in terms of certain actions (e.g., smoking, drinking, etc.). At its root, however, worldliness is an attitude of friendship toward, a desire for, and a wish to be recognized by the world system. As a result of this inner attitude, people indulge in worldly behavior. Sometimes these acts may not be wrong in themselves, but people do them to win the favor of the world system. In the 1980s, for example, rock star Michael Jackson popularized the style of wearing only one glove and leaving his tennis shoes untied. There was nothing inherently immoral in dressing that way, but doing so in imitation of Jackson was a conscious identification with a worldly lifestyle. Any act that arises from a worldly motive will identify you with the world system and thus hinder your love for God, your spiritual growth, and your Christian testimony.

Biblical Principle

In Chapters 3-5 we will look at key passages concerning each facet of separation. These are the major texts that teach the meaning of separation and set our guidelines for how it should be practiced. You need to be aware, though, that separation is not just an idea contained in a handful of isolated spots in the New Testament. Because the Bible is God's Word, it does not have to repeat a command constantly before we have to obey. A command given once by God is quite enough. Still, separatists are sometimes charged with "prooftexting," that is, citing a few verses (often out of context) to prop up a weak position. We will look at the context and teaching of each passage to show that it is in harmony with the overall teaching of God's Word. Furthermore, the cross-references to other passages and the Old Testament parallels indicate that separation is a theme throughout the Word of God.

Key New Testament Texts

I John 2:15-17

> Love not the world, neither the things that are in the world. If any man love the world, the love of the Father is not in him. For all that is in the world, the lust of the flesh, and the lust of the eyes, and the pride of life, is not of the Father, but is of the world. And the world passeth away, and the lust thereof: but he that doeth the will of God abideth for ever.

In these verses the apostle John gives all believers a categorical command to constantly avoid loving the world. Any person who makes the things of the world system the center of his interest and desire has exalted the world to a place of idolatrous worship. An idol is not simply a piece of stone or wood that someone kneels in front of. It is anything we regard as the supreme interest in our lives. A man who loves the world, John says, absolutely excludes the proper love for the Father from his life. Although God has made the material things of the world, we can pervert them into idols by regarding them as our supreme interest. Thus even the beauties of nature, art, music, or literature can become idols.

"The things that are in the world" can be the source of temptations in three general areas. "The lust of the flesh" is the desire that the flesh produces. It may be for an object that is good in itself, such as food (Matt. 4:3). But when food becomes more important than the will of God, it becomes an idol. "The lust of the eyes" is the desire for anything beautiful or attractive that can be exalted in place of God. It may be an object as good as a tree (Gen. 3:6). "The pride of life" is the selfish display of even good things that may replace the desire for God. Earl Nutz notes the difficulty of interpreting "pride of life." He characterizes it as "arrogance" and writes, "Arrogance and lust summarize the attitude of those who subscribe to the world's system."[1]

John tells us that the world system and all its appeals are passing away, but the believer who has made God the object of his existence—his supreme interest—will continue forever. God will make such a believer the heir of all things in Christ (Rev. 21:7).

II Corinthians 6:14–7:1

Be ye not unequally yoked together with unbelievers: for what fellowship hath righteousness with unrighteousness? and what communion hath light with darkness? And what concord hath Christ with Belial? or what part hath he that believeth with an infidel? And what agreement hath the temple of God with idols? for ye are the temple of the living God; as God hath said, I will dwell in them, and walk in them; and I will be their God, and they shall be my people. Wherefore come out from among them, and be ye separate, saith the Lord, and touch not the unclean thing: and I will receive you, and will be a Father unto you, and ye shall be my sons and daughters, saith the Lord Almighty. Having therefore these promises, dearly beloved, let us cleanse ourselves from all filthiness of the flesh and spirit, perfecting holiness in the fear of God.

In this passage the apostle Paul first states the principle that believers are not to be "unequally yoked together with unbelievers" (v. 14). He is probably alluding here to Deuteronomy 22:10, where God forbids plowing with an ox and a donkey yoked together. Such a mismatched pair cannot pull or plow effectively. Paul supports this principle with a series of contrasts that should be self-evident to Christians. Righteousness and unrighteousness as well as light and darkness have nothing in common (v. 14). Christ has no agreement with "Belial," a name from a Hebrew word meaning "worthless" and referring to Satan. A believer has no "part" with an unbeliever (v. 15). Finally, he contrasts the temple of God with idols (v. 16), explaining that believers are the temple of God.

Paul has warned of idolatry throughout the Corinthian letters (e.g., I Cor. 5:10-11; 8:1-10; 10:14, 19-28). As "the temple of God," believers enjoy a special relationship with God in which He dwells among them. The idea of setting up idols in the temple of God is abominable. Against this background Paul gives the command of the Lord: "Wherefore come out from among them, and be ye separate, saith the Lord" (v. 17). The result, he says, is that God will receive believers, and they shall be sons and daughters to Him. Paul defines for us what it means to "be ye separate" and to "touch not the unclean thing" by urging believers to obey this command in cleansing themselves "from all filthiness of the flesh and spirit" and in "perfecting holiness in the fear of God" (v. 1).

Thus we see that the practice of separation is grounded in the holiness of God. Paul lines out example after example of how the kingdom of God is in complete opposition to the world system. There is no basis of agreement between them. Describing Paul's five contrasts, Moritz says, "When the nature of the believer is contrasted with that of the unbeliever, it is incongruous that there should be any fellowship, sharing, harmony, part, or forming a coalition."[2] Because Christians are children of God and citizens of His kingdom, they must be separated *to* God and *from* sin and worldliness.

This passage, rightly called "the keystone passage in the New Testament which deals with separation,"[3] is one of the most cited as well as the most disputed in arguments over separation. Often it is used in the context of ecclesiastical separation, in part because it is addressed to a church and in part because the clear command "Come out from among them, and be ye separate" applies so well in urging believers and churches to leave apostate denominations. Also, Paul uses the temple as an image of the church (I Cor. 3:16-17; Eph. 2:21) as well as of the individual Christian (I Cor. 6:19). Critics of the separatist position protest against this use of the passage.[4] Their complaints center, however, in applying it to professing Christians. Eenigenburg states that "nowhere in the New Testament are some Christians given the privilege of declaring other professing Christians 'unbelievers'" so that they may separate from them.[5] Runia is subtler but questions the application: "How [this passage] is to be applied in the case of an unfaithful church must be decided by the teaching of the whole New Testament. A straightforward appeal to verse seventeen . . . in defense of separatism is an oversimplification of the issue."[6]

These critics generally recognize that separation from the world system is appropriate, even necessary. What they miss is the possibility that a church could become so identified with the world system that it has become part of that realm of unrighteousness, darkness, Belial, infidelity, and idolatry that God condemns.[7] God, for example, condemns "Mystery Babylon," the apostate religious system of the end times, and commands, "Come out of her, my people, that ye be not partakers of her sins, and that ye receive not of her plagues" (Rev. 18:4). Fundamentalist Chester Tulga seems almost bewildered by Christians who "contend that II Corinthians 6:14 forbids fellowship with idolaters but does not forbid fellowship with those who deny the fundamentals of the Christian faith."[8]

Paul elsewhere warns Timothy about "doctrines of devils" getting into the church (I Tim. 4:1).

Second Corinthians 6:14–7:1 does indeed deal primarily with the Christian's separation from the world system. But as we will see in the next chapter, separation from false teachers can also involve separating from the world system. For now, keep in mind the main teaching of II Corinthians 6:14–7:1, that God's kingdom is holy and therefore separate from Satan's realm. Therefore Christians, as citizens of His kingdom, are to imitate that holiness by clinging to God and spurning the world. The practice of separation rests "upon the basic fact of incompatibility between the like and the unlike."[9]

Ephesians 5:11

> And have no fellowship with the unfruitful works of darkness, but rather reprove them.

Perhaps the best place to start in understanding Paul's message in Ephesians 5:11 is to define our terms. The "unfruitful works of darkness" are defined earlier in verses 3-4: sexual immorality, impurity, greed, obscenity, and foolish talking or coarse joking. This list is not of all the works of darkness, of course, but more of a representative sampling. It is worth noting in light of I John 2:15-17 that Paul calls a man who practices these things an idolater (v. 5). These works of darkness are the supreme interest of his life.

Paul instructs the Ephesians not to "fellowship" with these works but to "reprove" them. The picture of "fellowshiping" with "works" may seem a strange one at first glance. But the idea is that we must not share or participate in such acts. By "reproof," Paul means to expose these acts. Hodge points out that this word is the same used in John 16:8 for the ministry of the Holy Spirit. "When the Spirit is said to reprove people of sin," he writes, "it means that he sheds such light on their sins that it reveals their true character and produces the consequent consciousness of guilt and pollution."[10] In contrasting fellowship with reproof, the apostle highlights the chasm that exists between those devoted to the "unfruitful works of darkness" and those devoted to the fruitful works of light.

Believers not only refuse to share in such sinful acts but also actively oppose them.

It is worth noting, however, that Paul forbids sharing in the works, and does not forbid interacting with the people who practice them. Christ pointed out the sin of the woman at the well of Samaria, but He nonetheless spoke with her about her need to drink from the "well of water springing up into everlasting life" (John 4:7-26). We may befriend the lost but not share in their works.

I Thessalonians 1:9
> For they themselves shew of us what manner of entering in we had unto you, and how ye turned to God from idols to serve the living and true God.

The opening of this verse, "for they themselves," refers to believers in "Macedonia and Achaia" (Greece; vv. 7-8). Paul, who is probably writing from Corinth, is hearing reports from these Greek Christians of the activities of the Thessalonian Christians. What are those activities? They are demonstrating the results of the ministry of Paul and the other missionaries in Thessalonica ("what manner of entering in we had unto you"). Specifically, the Thessalonians have "turned to God from idols to serve the living and true God."

The construction of this verse markedly contrasts serving idols with serving God. Hiebert points out that "turned" is the usual New Testament word for conversion.[11] To serve God is to move in a direction completely opposite from that of serving idols. Furthermore, the verse subtly describes the nature of idols. Since God is "living and true," then idols must be dead and false. The Thessalonians likely turned from literal idols. In light of the scriptural teaching on idolatry, however, anything that a person places before God in his interest will ultimately prove equally dead and false.

James 4:4
> Ye adulterers and adulteresses, know ye not that the friendship of the world is enmity with God? whosoever therefore will be a friend of the world is the enemy of God.

James intends his words to be shockingly blunt: "Ye adulterers and adulteresses." Adultery is sexual unfaithfulness in marriage.

James accuses his readers of spiritual adultery, of unfaithfulness to their relationship to God. He has warned them against lusts in the previous verses (1-3). This use of "lust" reinforces the imagery of adultery. Just as lust leads a partner in a marriage into unfaithfulness, so the lusts of the flesh can make Christians unfaithful to their God. Those who allow the world to ensnare their hearts away from God are committing spiritual adultery. James describes two allegiances that no one can reconcile. The world system is God's enemy; the friendship of the world is "enmity," literally *hatred,* toward God. Either people choose to be friends of the world and make themselves enemies of God, or they can be friends of God and therefore enemies of the world. There is no middle ground.

Old Testament Parallel

"Worldliness" was a constant problem for the people of Israel. When they rejected Samuel's sons as judges and asked for a king, their reason was "that we also may be like all the nations" (I Sam. 8:20). God taught His people to be separate from other people. This was not some arbitrary command, for holiness is expressed by separateness: "And ye shall be holy unto me: for I the Lord am holy, and have severed you from other people, that ye should be mine" (Lev. 20:26). When they consorted with the pagans, God sent prophets to condemn them for their evil associations (Isa. 30:1-17). Because of His grace and mercy, God called Israel to be His "peculiar treasure" and His "holy nation" (Exod. 19:5-6). Therefore, the people were to reflect that holy calling in their lives. This calling involved the separation from the false gods of the heathen and the prohibition of intermarriage with them. Yet it also involved experiencing the love, mercy, and faithfulness of their God (Deut. 7:1-11).

God sent judgment upon Israel when they apostatized from the Word of God and worshiped the gods of the heathen so that they became like the heathen, followed their practices, and intermarried with them. The book of Judges records a recurring cycle of unbelief and judgment because of such "worldliness." (See, e.g., Judg. 3:5-8.) God says that the specific reason for the fall of the Northern Kingdom of Israel was its following the ways of the ungodly nations (II Kings 17:6-8).

Proverbs has much to say about avoiding evil men (e.g., 4:14-19). God also promises blessing to those who do not associate with the wicked and their pagan lifestyle. The Psalms are filled with such promises. Psalm 1 contrasts these two ways: "Blessed is the man that walketh not in the counsel of the ungodly, nor standeth in the way of sinners, nor sitteth in the seat of the scornful. But his delight is in the law of the Lord; and in his law doth he meditate day and night. And he shall be like a tree planted by the rivers of water, that bringeth forth his fruit in his season; his leaf also shall not wither; and whatsoever he doeth shall prosper" (vv. 1-3).

Explanation and Application

Look over the passages we have discussed in this chapter. Note how God constantly reminds us of the gulf between His kingdom and the world system. Christ describes the normal relationship of the Christian to the world: "If the world hate you, ye know that it hated me before it hated you. If ye were of the world, the world would love his own: but because ye are not of the world, but I have chosen you out of the world, therefore the world hateth you" (John 15:18-19). The apostle John told the first-century Christians, "Marvel not, my brethren, if the world hate you" (I John 3:13). If this deep hatred between the world system and the Christian ceases, it is the Christian, not the world, who has changed.

Separation from the world is, therefore, first to recognize the completely evil character of the world. The Christian decides not to desire or to expect approval—or even fair treatment—from the world. Second, separation from the world means avoiding all actions that might fall into the category of worldliness as defined above. Sources of contamination from the world today include ungodly television programs, music, movies, and fashions. A main source of contamination that the Bible often specifically warns against is worldly friends (I Cor. 15:33). The Christian belongs to God and should turn his back on the sins of the world. The Christian will cast down its idols and reject all of its unbiblical ambitions and schemes. Keep in mind too that actions arise from the heart. It is the person whose heart belongs to God and is inclined toward holiness who truly understands what it means to forsake worldly behavior. Christians are not holy because they reject worldliness. They reject worldliness because they have been set apart by God in salvation and are being transformed by the Holy Spirit.

As we said in the last chapter, however, God's command to separate from the world does not mean that the Christian should isolate himself from society. Christians are to be the "salt of the earth" (Matt. 5:13). They are responsible to evangelize the world (Acts 1:8); therefore, separation from the world should by no means discourage earnest efforts to win the world to Christ. God Himself desires the salvation of the world (John 3:16; II Pet. 3:9).

Furthermore, separation from the world does not forbid association with worldly people in the course of legitimate daily work. Paul tells the Corinthians that he does not expect them to leave the world in order to avoid contamination from sinners (I Cor. 5:9-13). As we noted before, our Lord prays that believers be kept from the evil of the world, not removed from it (John 17:15). "As we have therefore opportunity," says the apostle Paul, "let us do good unto all men, especially unto them who are of the household of faith" (Gal. 6:10). The Christian may cooperate with unsaved people in beneficial community projects, such as electing worthy leaders or helping relieve the situation of the poor, the ill, and the underprivileged. In such efforts, though, the Christian must be careful not to make it appear as though unsaved people are Christians. Nor should these efforts promote any organization that is using social or political efforts to further unbiblical causes. Biblical characters such as Joseph, Daniel, and Nehemiah are examples of men who worked in pagan environments while remaining true to God.

Finally, we should note the charge of legalism that is often laid against those who stress separation from the world. Defined biblically, legalism is a serious heresy. Basically, it is trying to earn merit with God by performing good works. Paul dealt with this problem in his epistle to the Galatians. In Galatia false teachers were saying that men could be justified (Gal. 2:16) or sanctified (3:1-5) by performing good works, in this case following the Mosaic law. Paul would have no part of such a teaching.

As we said before, we do not become more holy by doing certain things; actions express what is in our hearts. Those who use the term *legalism* against Christians who practice separation probably do not mean it in this technical sense, however. Rather they seem to use it to mean requiring standards of behavior that have no basis in the Bible.[12] Certainly, there is a danger in requiring people to dress a certain way or in forbidding some action without any command of the Lord. For example, around 1900 the Church of God (Anderson, Indiana) underwent a major fight over worldliness. The cause of this bitter struggle? Wearing neckties. Eventually, part of the anti-necktie faction founded its own church.[13] Fundamentalists should be careful about focusing on unscriptural standards.

But, as Ken Pulliam says, "Christian Standards are not Legalism." He recognizes the dangers of mindlessly imposing rules of conduct: Christians who go "through the motions" but have "no real joy or delight in serving the Lord," or who are hypocrites like the Pharisees, or who are so isolated that they have no witness to the world.[14] But God imposes certain standards of conduct on His people. (See, e.g., Eph. 4:22-32; Col. 3:8-17; I Tim. 3:2-13.) Our reply is similar to the one we made in the last chapter about the charge of schism. While we should be careful in imposing standards to make sure they are scriptural ones, obeying God's Word can never be the sin of legalism.

Purposes

Christians, therefore, separate from the world and from worldliness for the following reasons:

1. To avoid the ever-present danger of contamination by the world (I Cor. 11:32; 15:33; II Cor. 11:3; I Thess. 4:5; I Pet. 2:12).

2. To maintain close fellowship with God (John 15:15; James 4:4).

3. To base their lives on that which is enduring (John 15:16).

4. To make clear to Christians and non-Christians alike by their actions that they belong to God, not to the world (Isa. 43:21; I Thess. 5:22; I Pet. 2:9).

5. To avoid sin (James 4:17).

Can you see how these purposes contribute to our overall goal of Christlikeness for the believer? Jesus Christ was sinless; there was certainly no hint of "worldliness" about Him. He lived to reveal His Father to the world, and He maintained a close fellowship with the Father. Christ's focus was the eternal will of God, not temporal, temporary advantage or comfort. Jesus overcame "the lust of the flesh, and the lust of the eyes, and the pride of life" in His temptation by Satan (Matt. 4:1-11; Luke 4:1-13). Is this not the pattern we wish to follow?

Conclusion

Christians who practice personal separation demonstrate in conduct and attitude a strict obedience to God and His Word. In addition, they testify to the world of their inner love for God and their desire to be like Him. Separation has what may be called a "negative" side: believers refuse to look and act like the world because they have no desire for the world. Consider this fact as well—every human is born in sin. From our conception, we are all subjects of Satan's world system. Salvation from sin is our separation from that world. The pull of the flesh constantly wars against separation in the Christian's life by inducing him to sin. The Christian therefore has to oppose the flesh to exercise separation.

There is a positive side too: the believer is to be more like Christ. You should not view separation as some kind of sacrifice you make for God. Rather it is a submission to God's wisdom, a testimony to your faith that He knows what is best for you. Certainly, you should not see separation as a way to earn God's favor. "Salvation does not begin with giving up something but with receiving Someone."[15] God has already showed the Christian enormous favor in saving him. He, the Almighty, has entered into a personal relationship with a mere human. Separation is but one of our responses to God for His goodness toward us. Separation properly practiced is, in fact, an act of worship.

Separation from False Teachers
Chapter 4

We mentioned in Chapter 1 that many discussions of separation divide the topic into personal and ecclesiastical separation. Generally, those who follow this approach would see the topic in the previous chapter—separation from the world—as an expression of personal separation. This chapter—separating from false teachers—focuses more on ecclesiastical separation. Positively, ecclesiastical separation involves identification with groups faithful to the truth and practice of God's Word. Negatively, it is the refusal to be identified with any teacher, church, denomination, or other religious organization that does not hold to and contend for the fundamentals of the Faith concerning the Bible, Christ, and salvation.

Yet we should not draw hard-and-fast lines between "kinds" of separation. Sin does not always fall into neat categories. Although we often speak of worldliness and the world system in connection with personal separation, the concepts are also important in discussing ecclesiastical separation. Douglas McLachlan defines ecclesiastical separation as "radical non-conformity to Babel," that is, a refusal to conform to the "satanic" religious pattern of the world system.[1] The famous separation passage "Wherefore come out from among them, and be ye separate, saith the Lord" (II Cor. 6:17) is an allusion to Isaiah 52:11. In that verse God is calling His people out of literal Babylon, and He specifically charges the priests (those "that bear the vessels of the Lord") to be clean.

Regardless of whether we can pigeonhole sins into certain classifications, we need to understand the danger of false teaching. If it is indeed the religious belief of the world system (and it is), then false teaching is of Satan and is a threat to the souls of men. Christians must guard themselves against it, and they must warn others. "Thus saith the Lord of hosts, Hearken not unto the words of the prophets that prophesy unto you: they make you vain: they speak a vision of their own heart, and not out of the mouth of the Lord" (Jer. 23:16).

Definitions

False Teacher: Someone who professes to be a Christian but who attempts to deceive the church by false doctrine is a false teacher. He is described in Scripture as a wolf in sheep's clothing, who is to be judged on the basis of his works (doctrinal teaching and its effects) and not merely on his profession (Matt. 7:15-20; Titus 1:16). Although such deceivers give the appearance of being angels of light and ministers of righteousness, the Bible calls them false apostles, deceitful workers (II Cor. 11:13-15), servants of corruption (II Pet. 2:19), ungodly men (Jude 4), filthy dreamers (Jude 8), and mockers (Jude 18). We normally presume such a person is unregenerate, although we do not always know for sure. Commenting on Acts 20:29-30, Randy Jaeggli says, "These are wolves dressed up like sheep, or sheep who are acting like wolves (sometimes it is hard to tell the difference)."[2] Regardless of his personal standing with God, such a person is unquestionably teaching doctrine that threatens the eternal well-being of our souls.

Fundamental Doctrine: A fundamental doctrine is a clear scriptural teaching that the Bible itself indicates is an important truth of Christianity. It is a teaching so essential to Christianity that it cannot be denied without destroying Christianity. The fundamentals of the Faith do not include those points of doctrine that are matters of particular interpretation. Good men have differed with each other on many points of doctrine, but they agree on the fundamentals. There can be no room for difference of opinion concerning the full inspiration, inerrancy, and authority of the Bible; the virgin birth of Christ; His essential deity and proper humanity; His absolute sinlessness; His power to save the sinner through His substitutionary death on the cross; His bodily resurrection; His personal return; and the reality of heaven and hell.

Of course, to distinguish between what is an essential of the Faith and what is a matter of interpretation requires spiritual discernment. True teachers of the Word have sometimes disagreed concerning the interpretation of specific Scripture relating to church ordinances or the details associated with Christ's return. Rolland McCune lists several teachings that he sees as "doctrinal non-issues" in Fundamentalism, including preference for certain families of biblical manuscripts, Calvinism and Arminianism, questions of church polity, and differing systems of prophetic interpretation.[3] This is not to say that such issues are unimportant, but they are not fundamental to the Christian faith.

Biblical Principle
Key New Testament Texts

Galatians 1:8-9

> But though we, or an angel from heaven, preach any other gospel unto you than that which we have preached unto you, let him be accursed. As we said before, so say I now again, If any man preach any other gospel unto you than that ye have received, let him be accursed.

Satan seeks to corrupt Christ's church through false ministers who preach a false message. Having warned against "another gospel: which is not another" (vv. 6-7), Paul adamantly teaches that no change can be introduced into the apostolic gospel and states this teaching in unmistakably strong terms.

Let us begin by considering what Paul means by "another gospel." According to passages such as Luke 24:44-47 and I Corinthians 15:1-8, the gospel includes teachings such as Christ's death for our sins, His resurrection, and the forgiveness of sin only through Him. These truths are certainly central teachings of the gospel. In Galatians, however, Paul specifically charges the Galatian believers with turning from the grace of Christ (v. 6). He is criticizing the heresy of legalism that we mentioned in the previous chapter. False teachers were saying that believers must follow the Mosaic law to be saved (2:16; 3:1-5). This legalism is "another gospel."

In verses 6-7 Paul uses two different words for "another" in "*another* gospel, which is not *another*." The first means "something entirely different," and the second means "something of the same kind." These teachers presented a "gospel" that had nothing in common with the true gospel. It is "so different from Paul's message that it constitutes . . . 'a different "gospel" '—and therefore, in fact, no gospel at all, since there can be no 'other gospel.' "[4]

If any human being, or even an angel from heaven, preaches another gospel (another of a different kind), Paul prays that he should be accursed. Machen points out that Paul is not just saying that these false teachers have no right to change the gospel; *no one* has the right to change it.[5] Martin Luther said, "That which does not teach Christ is not apostolic, even if Peter and Paul be the teachers. On the other hand, that which does teach Christ is apostolic, even if Judas, Annas, Pilate or Herod should propound it."[6] Machen also notes that Paul was willing to endure people preaching the true gospel for bad motives (Phil. 1:15-18), but he would not endure someone preaching a "bad gospel," even with good intentions.[7]

The word "accursed" is *anathema,* which originally had the meaning of "offering." The idea is something being handed over to God, in this case, handed over for judgment. Paul almost certainly meant that such teachers should be excluded from the church, but more than that they are to be given over to a severe judgment at God's hands. Boice says that the literal sense is "Let them be damned" and that anybody, even Paul himself, is included.[8] This emphatic language demonstrates the fervor of Paul's attitude toward those who would modify any part of the gospel he preached.

II John 9-11

> Whosoever transgresseth, and abideth not in the doctrine of Christ, hath not God. He that abideth in the doctrine of Christ, he hath both the Father and the Son. If there come any unto you, and bring not this doctrine, receive him not into your house, neither bid him God speed: for he that biddeth him God speed is partaker of his evil deeds.

The apostle John gives one of the Bible's sternest warnings concerning false teachers in II John 9-11. He has just said (v. 7) that "many deceivers are entered into the world, who confess not that Jesus Christ is come in the flesh." Such a person "is a deceiver and an antichrist." The word *antichrist* here does not refer to the Beast of the end times (Rev. 13:1-10) but refers to anyone who sets himself against Christ and attempts to take the place of Christ. An antichrist, then, reflects the character of Satan.

John describes the consequences of such false teachings. Anyone who goes beyond and will not continue abiding in the biblical doctrine of Christ has abandoned God. The word translated "transgresseth" perhaps should be instead a word translated "progresses." These teachers claimed to have "progressed" in their teaching of Christ to a higher level. "Such progress beyond the revelation in Christ, however, was not spiritual advancement but a fatal plunge into spiritual darkness."[9]

What is the "doctrine of Christ" that they are denying? The most obvious idea, based on the words "confess not that Jesus Christ is come in the flesh" in verse 7, is that they are denying the real incarnation of Jesus as truly human. There was an early heresy called Docetism that denied that Jesus had a real body and was a sort of ghost who only appeared to be human. Other teachings about Christ that John stressed in his writings against false teachers are that Jesus is the Messiah ("the Christ"; I John 2:22) and that Jesus is the Son of God (I John 2:23). The tense of the verb "is come" in verse 7 could imply that these teachers are denying the Second Coming of Christ. All of these are essential teachings concerning Christ.

We need not extract particular doctrinal teachings from the passage, though. John says that believers must continue abiding in the doctrine of Christ to have fellowship with the Father and the Son. The "doctrine of Christ" is the Bible's whole teaching concerning who Jesus is and what He has done. The true teacher is not just someone who believes certain truths about Jesus. He accepts the entire person and work of Christ. Peter Masters notes, "We are taught that any Christian teacher who does not truly believe in Christ as the incarnate Saviour, is devoid of any personal relationship with God." Masters argues that this is not simply a matter of whether a teacher believes in the incarnation but whether such a teacher is genuinely converted.[10]

Because denying the doctrine of Christ is so seriously wrong, believers are to have nothing to do with anyone who claims authority as a teacher but who is not sound concerning the Bible's teaching about Christ. Christians should not give such a person religious recognition of any kind. They should not do anything that could be construed as recognizing his false teaching or aiding him in his falsehood. To do so would mean that believers share in his wrongdoing. To pray for God's blessing on such a false teacher would be asking God to bless apostasy and heresy. Those who wish the false teacher well or help him on his way are aiding in the destruction of souls by false teaching. Critics often accuse Fundamentalists of being unloving for refusing to work with liberals, but in reality they are properly loving the souls of others by refusing to promote destructive heresy.

Romans 16:17-18

> Now I beseech you, brethren, mark them which cause divisions and offences contrary to the doctrine which ye have learned; and avoid them. For they that are such serve not our Lord Jesus Christ, but their own belly; and by good words and fair speeches deceive the hearts of the simple.

At the conclusion of his epistle to the Romans, Paul urges his readers to deal wisely with false teachers. He says to "mark them," that is, watch out or be on the lookout for them. The reason for watching is that they "cause divisions and offences that are contrary to the doctrine which you have learned." It is not just that the divisions themselves are contrary to "the doctrine" (although that is partly true). The divisions are caused by the false teachings. The Roman Christians' standard for judging these false teachings is "the doctrine which ye have learned." Paul is not referring to some teaching he has given them. As Morris points out, Paul had not yet been to Rome and this is his first contact with this church.[11] The doctrine is the Christian faith that they have embraced. The Roman Christians are to "avoid" such teachers, to stay away from them altogether. Christians achieve true unity only by eliminating the errors that cause divisions, not by overlooking the errors.

Paul does not identify the group he is warning against, but verse 18 makes clear that these are false teachers. They serve their "belly" (their own selfish appetites) instead of Christ. These teachers speak "good words" and give "fair speeches" but they deceive "the simple," the naive and uninformed. The false teachers are slickly eloquent, but their teaching is poisonous in its effect.

I Timothy 6:20-21

> O Timothy, keep that which is committed to thy trust, avoiding profane and vain babblings, and oppositions of science falsely so called: which some professing have erred concerning the faith. Grace be with thee. Amen.

In I Timothy 6:20-21 Paul offers the last of a series of warnings he has given Timothy concerning false teaching (1:3-7, 18-21; 4:1-5; 6:3-5). Positively, he tells Timothy to "keep that which is committed to thy trust." Timothy is to guard what has been deposited with him, like someone guarding a treasure. (Paul uses similar language in II Tim. 1:14.) The context of I Timothy makes evident that what has been entrusted to Timothy is "sound doctrine" (I Tim. 1:10; 4:6, 16; 6:3).

Negatively, Timothy is to guard this treasure by "avoiding profane and vain babblings, and oppositions of science falsely so called." In other places as well Paul describes the teaching of false teachers as pointless chattering that leads only to ungodliness (I Tim. 1:6; 4:7; II Tim. 2:16). The word translated "science" is normally translated "knowledge" in the New Testament. The false teachers claim that they have true knowledge. Paul shows that they do not. He tells Timothy that what these teachers say is in opposition to the truth that Timothy guards. Furthermore, Timothy is to turn from such teaching in order to protect the truth entrusted to him.

Paul highlights the danger of these teachings by stating that those who profess these teachings have "erred concerning"—that is, turned aside or wandered from—the Faith. This is not a simple difference of opinion; this is a difference between truth and error. The fate of souls rests on this difference.

Revelation 2:2, 6, 14-16

> I know thy works, and thy labour, and thy patience, and how
> thou canst not bear them which are evil: and thou hast tried
> them which say they are apostles, and are not, and hast found
> them liars. . . . But this thou hast, that thou hatest the deeds of
> the Nicolaitanes, which I also hate. . . .
>
> But I have a few things against thee, because thou hast
> there them that hold the doctrine of Balaam, who taught Balac
> to cast a stumbling block before the children of Israel, to eat
> things sacrificed unto idols, and to commit fornication. So hast
> thou also them that hold the doctrine of the Nicolaitanes, which
> thing I hate. Repent; or else I will come unto thee quickly, and
> will fight against them with the sword of my mouth.

Chapters 2-3 of the Book of Revelation contain seven letters
that Jesus addresses to seven different churches in Asia Minor. In
chapter 2, Christ addresses the churches at Ephesus (vv. 1-7) and
Pergamum (vv. 12-17). Christ praises the church at Ephesus for
resisting false teaching and condemns the church at Pergamum for
tolerating it. The Ephesians had tested the teaching and rejected it.
The believers at Pergamum, although not denying the Faith (v. 13),
had permitted false teaching in their ranks and needed to repent.

The teaching Christ condemns in these churches is that of the
"Nicolaitanes." We have no certain knowledge of this group. The
earliest references in the church fathers say that this group taught
that Christians could "lead lives of unrestrained indulgence."[12]
Christ describes their teaching as "the doctrine of Balaam." (Verse
15 translates more literally, "And thus you are likewise having
those who hold the teaching of the Nicolaitanes." The Nicolaitans
hold to the same teaching described in verse 14, not a different one,
as we might think from a casual reading of the KJV.)

Balaam is best known as the greedy prophet in Numbers 22-24,
who blessed the children of Israel almost against his will. The
incident Christ refers to, however, took place soon afterwards.
Numbers 25 describes how the Israelites joined in the immoral
pagan worship of the Midianites and began to intermarry with the
Midianites. Numbers 31:16 tells us that it was Balaam who advised

King Balak of the Midianites to try this policy of "If you can't beat them, get them to join you." Like Balaam, these false teachers urged compromise with idolatry by eating meat sacrificed to idols. (See Paul's warnings about this practice in I Cor. 8:1-13; 10:14-33.) Furthermore, they "commit fornication." This could be a reference to spiritual unfaithfulness (see James 4:4). It is possible, though, that some people in the church at Pergamum were actually teaching that Christians could indulge in sexual immorality, perhaps in connection with the pagan temples. Jude warns of false teachers who change "the grace of our God into lasciviousness" (Jude 4).

Note how clear is Christ's attitude toward false teaching. He says that He hates both the deeds (v. 6) and the doctrines (v. 15) of the Nicolaitans. The only solution for the church at Pergamum is to repent of this false teaching, or Christ Himself will come to fight against those who hold it.

Old Testament Parallel

The presence of false prophets among the people of God in the Old Testament was a common problem (II Pet. 2:1), and the condemnation of such teachers was a constant theme. God taught His people that they were to reject a false prophet totally. If what he predicted did not happen, they would know he was false (Deut. 18:20-22). Even should he correctly predict the future and verify it with a miracle, the people would know that he was a false prophet if he tried to lead them astray from the true God (Deut. 13:1-5). The people judged teachers by their actions and by the content of their teaching. Purity of doctrine must accompany purity of life.

Jeremiah and Ezekiel faced the problem of false prophets during their times (Jer. 23; Ezek. 13). These false teachers discouraged backslidden people from repenting by telling them that peace was on the way. As a result of their lies, many perished. Of course, Jeremiah and Ezekiel preached against these deceivers. Other Old Testament prophets also used strong language to condemn false prophets (I Kings 22:25; Isa. 28:7; Hos. 4:5; Mic. 2:6-8, 11; Zeph. 3:4). All of God's prophets strongly denounced false worship. They condemned any effort by the Israelites to combine their religious practices with those of the nations around them.

Explanation and Application

We saw in the last chapter that there is an absolute distinction between the kingdom of God and the world system. The passages discussed in this chapter demonstrate the same divergence between the true doctrine of Christ and false teaching. They have nothing in common. Just as Paul warned the Ephesian elders that they would have problems with false teachers (Acts 20:29-31), so believers today can expect to face problems with such people. How do Christians deal with false teachers?

First, Christians must judge all doctrinal teaching in the light of Scripture. If a preacher or a teacher of God's people denies clear scriptural teaching and practice, true believers should recognize him as a false teacher.

Second, it is necessary to rebuke the false teachers in order to deliver those who have been influenced by their teaching. This rebuke should be as strong as those used by Christ (Matt. 23:13-36) and by His apostles (Gal. 1:9; 5:12).

Third, all conduct toward false teachers should be based upon the truth that an apostate gets only progressively worse in his doctrine (II Tim. 3:13) and that there is no scriptural evidence that an apostate ever returns to Christ (Heb. 6:4-6). An apostate has deliberately rejected revealed truth. Such false teachers must be expelled from the church and from any positions of influence involving a religious institution, publication, or missionary society.

Finally, when expelling such men is impossible because the majority of the people in the church, society, or institution are supporting them, it then becomes necessary for believers to withdraw from that group. Undoubtedly, it is this point of separation that is the most controversial. Few conservative Christians question the legitimacy of separating from outright apostasy. Eenigenburg, writing against separatism, comes close to denying separation from apostasy, but even he is willing to admit the possibility.[13] Instead critics offer qualifications and limitations to the idea of separation. Runia is typical in saying that believers should not tolerate heresy in the church but they should expel it, not withdraw from the church.[14] Ronald Nash criticizes conservatives for leaving denominations whenever they fell into a minority and were unable to expel false teachers. They should have hung on, he says, to maintain their influence and perhaps win later on.[15]

Some claim that there is not a clear New Testament example of a faction withdrawing from a church for scriptural reasons, although Runia allows that in the first century "the New Testament church *separates itself from the Jewish church.*"[16] But the situation at that time did not require the scriptural principle to be applied in that way. Opponents of separation seem to say that if expulsion fails, then the believers who lose a battle must simply tolerate serious error in their midst. This argument, however, flies in the face of the passages we studied in this chapter. Christians are to avoid false teaching (Rom. 16:17) and refuse to have fellowship with it (II John 9-11). Expelling the error is the first course of action we should take, but if a majority refuses to do so, then the minority must obey the scriptural principle of refusing to fellowship with error by withdrawing.

A common plea against such separation is to appeal to the parable of the wheat and the tares (Matt. 13:24-30, 36-43).[17] The basic argument is that the church is a mixed multitude, containing both wheat (true Christians) and tares (unregenerate people posing as Christians). Jesus says that the two should remain mixed until the final judgment, when He will reveal which believers are true and which are spurious. Therefore, Christians should not try to separate the wheat from the tares themselves but should endure this mixed condition. There is a legitimate application of this idea (as we will see in a moment), but there are major problems in this manner of presenting it. The biggest difficulty is that Jesus says, "The field is the *world*" (v. 38), not the church. Clearly, this world is a mixture of the saved and the unsaved, and Christians cannot use force to uproot the unbelievers. In addition, the interpretation of this parable cannot be used to invalidate God's commands to put away false teaching. As we have said before, Scripture cannot contradict Scripture.

We should mention three cautions concerning separation from false teaching. First, separation from false teachers does not involve separation from ordinary hypocrites—church members who secretly do not believe what they profess to believe. God has not called us to judge the motives of others. If people believe false doctrine but give no outward sign of their attitude and do not teach anything false to other members of the church, they might remain in the church until they do manifest themselves as "tares." Judas, one of the twelve chosen by Christ, remained with the group until Christ's death. He never revealed himself to the disciples as a false teacher or even as an unconverted man. Christians cannot know someone's heart and cannot act until a person gives open evidence that he is a false teacher.

Second, in this regard, we must remember that only God knows the heart of a false teacher. It is perhaps possible that some who proclaim apostate teaching are themselves deceived.[18] A true apostate is without hope, but we cannot always know who is a true apostate. After warning Timothy against false teachers, Paul admonished Timothy to "be gentle unto all men, apt to teach, patient, in meekness instructing those that oppose themselves; if God peradventure will give them repentance to the acknowledging of the truth" (II Tim. 2:24-25). Nevertheless, we must treat anyone who holds to apostate teaching as though he were an apostate himself. Immediately after warning Timothy to be gentle, Paul goes on to describe false teachers in pointed terms and tells the younger man, "from such turn away" (II Tim. 3:5). For the protection of the church, we must expel such teachers. If indeed such a man is merely deceived, expulsion may be a means of confronting him with the truth.

Third, separation from false teachers does not involve the rejection of a novice who may express some views contrary to fundamental doctrine. If the novice submits himself to correction and chooses to obey the teaching of Scripture, he should not be regarded as a false teacher.

Purposes

The Christian separates from false teachers and their teaching for the following reasons:

1. To maintain the doctrinal integrity of the church (I Tim. 3:15; Jude 12).

2. To protect the sheep from error that not only inhibits spiritual growth but also can destroy faith (Matt. 7:15; Acts 20:28; II Tim. 2:18; Titus 1:11; II Pet. 2:1-2).

We may again see a pattern of Christlikeness here. It is Christ's purpose to save and to sanctify the church "that he might present it to himself a glorious church, not having spot, or wrinkle, or any such thing; but that it should be holy and without blemish" (Eph. 5:27). Furthermore, Christ is the Good Shepherd (John 10). He knows His sheep and they know Him, and He protects them, lays down His life for them, and gives them abundant life; He protects His flock from the wolves. Peter tells the leaders of the church to "feed [literally, *shepherd*] the flock of God" as their duty before "the chief Shepherd," Jesus Christ (I Pet. 5:1-4).

Conclusion

Obeying God is often not easy, and separation from false teachers requires effort. Believers must be alert to the danger of false teaching and be discerning about what they hear—and what they accept. Christians must be courageous enough to denounce error and courageous enough to be willing either to expel the error or (what can be harder) to leave a group if expulsion fails. But the reward of obedience is rich. After commanding, "Wherefore come out from among them, and be ye separate," the Lord promises, "And I will receive you, and will be a Father unto you, and ye shall be my sons and daughters" (II Cor. 6:17-18).

Separation from Disobedient Christians
Chapter 5

"As long as biblical separation is discussed on a theoretical level, many Christians do not question its importance," writes Fred Moritz. "When separation is applied in practice to people and institutions they know, however, some believers bristle."[1] With no aspect of separation is this observation truer than in separation from disobedient brethren. Most Christians will acknowledge at least the concept of separation from worldliness or apostasy. But many argue vehemently against the very idea of separation from other Christians. Typical of this position is E. J. Carnell, who writes, "Christian fellowship repudiates *any* separation of brother from brother in the community of faith."[2] Our purpose in this chapter is to show that, on the contrary, the Bible does at times command such separation.

Yet it would be good to note some cautions as we begin. When we speak of "disobedient brethren," we mean the willful practice of disobedience. No believer is perfect, and all Christians disobey God at some point. We all need God's grace to triumph over the power of sin in our lives, and we need love and discernment to deal with and help other Christians in their weakness. Separation should never eliminate Christian sympathy from our hearts. The situation with which we are dealing in this chapter is a time when professing Christians are consistently violating a biblical command on some point. Furthermore, having been confronted about that activity, they refuse to repent. The Scripture offers clear teaching on this point. Even then, the goal of separation is not only the purity of the church but also the restoration of the brother. Through separation we wish to bring a Christian brother back into the full fellowship he should enjoy with other believers in Jesus Christ.

Separation from disobedient Christians can involve personal separation (a brother refusing to forsake some form of worldliness) or ecclesiastical separation (refusing to forsake some form of false teaching or unscriptural practice). But since it is usually practiced as an exercise of church discipline, we normally think of it as a form of ecclesiastical separation. Regardless of how we classify the practice, we must not underestimate the importance of this teaching.

Definitions

Disobedient Brother: A professing Christian who deliberately refuses to change some aspect of his conduct to conform to the clear teaching of Scripture is a disobedient brother. Our attitude will differ from that we would take with a false teacher because the disobedient brother has, we presume, faith in Christ's saving work. However, he refuses to cease from his disobedient practice.

Discipline in the Church: Church discipline is action taken by the body of believers to correct the disobedience of one of its members. Anyone who loves the brethren desires to see them do right (I Cor. 13:6). Proper church discipline results in the building up of the church, not in its destruction (II Cor. 13:10). The goal of such discipline is to reclaim the disobedient Christian (Matt. 18:15).

Biblical Principle
Key New Testament Texts
Matthew 18:15-17

> Moreover if thy brother shall trespass against thee, go and tell him his fault between thee and him alone: if he shall hear thee, thou hast gained thy brother. But if he will not hear thee, then take with thee one or two more, that in the mouth of two or three witnesses every word may be established. And if he shall neglect to hear them, tell it unto the church: but if he neglect to hear the church, let him be unto thee as an heathen man and a publican.

Only twice do the Gospels record teachings by Jesus concerning the church. In Matthew 16:18-19 He speaks of the foundation and building of His church. In Matthew 18:15-17 He speaks of discipline within that church.

In clear order, Jesus outlines the procedure that believers should follow in church discipline. Christ says that if your brother sins against you in some way, you must first go to him. Perhaps that will settle matters immediately and you will have "gained thy brother." If this visit does not settle the matter, then, second, you are to go back with one or two witnesses and discuss the matter again. The purpose of the witnesses would seem to be to report on this encounter to the church and to ensure that the actions and attitudes of the brother are accurately reported. (See Deut. 19:15.) Separation should never be based on rumor or talebearing. If this meeting fails, then you are to bring the questions before the whole church (that is, the local assembly of believers). If the brother refuses to heed the church, that body must exclude him and treat him as "an heathen man and a publican," that is, a pagan and a tax collector. Jews would have nothing to do with Gentiles or with tax collectors (even those who were themselves Jews). Christ's teaching is that the church is to break fellowship with the offender and treat him as though he were not part of the church.

A final point to keep in mind is that immediately after Christ gives this teaching, Peter asks how often he should forgive someone who sins against him. Christ replies "seventy times seven" and tells the parable of the unforgiving servant (vv. 21-35). When Christians are thinking of how much they should forgive an offending brother, they should keep in mind how much God has forgiven them. If a brother refuses to repent, he should be treated as an unregenerate man, but if he asks forgiveness, then believers are to welcome him back.

I Corinthians 5:1-13

> It is reported commonly that there is fornication among you, and such fornication as is not so much as named among the Gentiles, that one should have his father's wife. And ye are puffed up, and have not rather mourned, that he that hath done this deed might be taken away from among you. For I verily, as absent in body, but present in spirit, have judged already, as though I were present, concerning him that hath so done this deed, in the name of our Lord Jesus Christ, when ye are gathered together, and my spirit, with the power of our Lord Jesus Christ, to deliver such an one unto Satan for the destruction of the flesh, that the spirit may be saved in the day of the Lord Jesus.
>
> Your glorying is not good. Know ye not that a little leaven leaveneth the whole lump? Purge out therefore the old leaven,

that ye may be a new lump, as ye are unleavened. For even Christ our passover is sacrificed for us: therefore let us keep the feast, not with old leaven, neither with the leaven of malice and wickedness; but with the unleavened bread of sincerity and truth.

I wrote unto you in an epistle not to company with fornicators: yet not altogether with the fornicators of this world, or with the covetous, or extortioners, or with idolaters; for then must ye needs go out of the world. But now I have written unto you not to keep company, if any man that is called a brother be a fornicator, or covetous, or an idolater, or a railer, or a drunkard, or an extortioner; with such an one no not to eat. For what have I to do to judge them also that are without? do not ye judge them that are within? But them that are without God judgeth. Therefore put away from among yourselves that wicked person.

If Matthew 18:15-18 represents the concept of church discipline, then this passage reflects its practice. The apostle Paul seriously rebukes the Corinthians for failing to discipline one of their number who is involved in incest, probably with his stepmother. Paul writes sternly to them, commanding that the guilty person "be taken away from among you" (v. 2). He is to be delivered "unto Satan for the destruction of the flesh, that the spirit may be saved in the day of the Lord Jesus" (v. 5). Paul uses the same language in I Timothy 1:20 concerning Hymenaeus and Alexander. There is some debate about the exact meaning of this phrase.[3] However, its connection with "be taken away from among you" means that it refers at least partly to excluding such a person from the church. The goal of discipline for the one being excluded is to restore him.

Paul explains the danger of this situation to the church at Corinth. He uses the imagery of leaven, or yeast, in cooking (vv. 6-8). A little bit of yeast spreads through an entire lump of dough, affecting the whole lump and causing it all to rise. So, Paul says, will be the effect of sin. If the church tolerates the practice of sin by one member, that sin will affect the whole body. Having been cleansed from sin by Christ, our desire should then be to be free of sin in this life. The goal of discipline for the church is purity—to cleanse itself from sin.

Paul does not encourage believers to leave the world by walling themselves up in a monastery (v. 10). But he does warn that believers must not keep company with someone whose doctrine or practice contradicts scriptural standards (v. 11). The offenses Paul lists (vv. 10-11) are mostly moral offenses, such as sexual immorality, covetousness, and drunkenness. However, he also includes idolatry, which is, as Moritz notes, "separation from a disobedient brother . . . on doctrinal as well as moral grounds."[4] It is important to keep this point in mind as we discuss separation from other Christians. Paul concludes the chapter by commanding, "Therefore put away from among yourselves that wicked person" (v. 13). The church may not stand by and watch the disobedient brother continue his downward course without warning. Rather the Corinthian assembly is to warn him in an attempt to turn him from his destructive course. But until he repents, believers are not to have fellowship with him.

There is a footnote to this passage. In II Corinthians 2:5-11 Paul discusses an individual who had sinned, had been disciplined by the church, and had repented. We have no way of knowing whether this is the same person that Paul condemns in I Corinthians 5. But Paul nonetheless teaches clearly that a Christian who repents after church discipline is to be welcomed back without hesitation.

II Thessalonians 3:6, 14-15

> Now we command you, brethren, in the name of our Lord Jesus Christ, that ye withdraw yourselves from every brother that walketh disorderly, and not after the tradition which he received of us. . . . And if any man obey not our word by this epistle, note that man, and have no company with him, that he may be ashamed. Yet count him not as an enemy, but admonish him as a brother.

The apostle commands believers to "withdraw . . . from every brother" who "walketh disorderly, and not after the tradition" received from the apostles. Central questions in understanding this passage are the meanings of "withdraw," "disorderly," and "tradition."

"Withdraw . . . from" is simply to separate from, to withhold fellowship from. Morris argues, "In light of v. 15 this does not mean 'abstain from all intercourse,' but it stands for the withholding of intimate fellowship. . . . They had to be made to see that complete fellowship is possible only when there is complete harmony."[5]

The word translated "disorderly" originally had the meaning of being out of line, like a soldier who breaks rank from a march. By Paul's time it had acquired a meaning of idleness.[6] Paul had warned about this matter in his earlier epistle (I Thess. 5:14). In this passage he confronts those Christians who apparently claimed that the Lord's return was so imminent that they could stop working, and they had become meddlers as a result (vv. 7-12). Paul says "that if any would not work, neither should he eat" (v. 10) and tells the Thessalonians to withdraw from those Christians who refuse to obey.

Paul does not leave the reader to wonder what "tradition" is; it refers to instruction he has given them. In this specific instance, Paul was instructing them as he had in I Thessalonians 4:11 that they should work to support themselves. But "tradition" means more than that. In II Thessalonians 2:15 the apostle clearly declares the traditions to be his own teaching, whether by word or by epistle. In that verse Paul is contrasting the Christian message with the false teaching prevalent in the last days (vv. 2-12). When he tells them to "hold the traditions" in verse 15, he is referring to the great truths of salvation, election, sanctification, and the gospel that he mentions in verses 13-14. If any brother's practice or teaching in *any* point does not agree with the teaching of Scripture, believers are to withdraw from him.

Lest any believer fail to realize the importance of this discipline, the apostle repeats the command at the end of chapter 3. If any man will not obey the teaching in Paul's epistles, Christians should "note that man, and have no company with him, that he may be ashamed" (II Thess. 3:14). To allow him to continue in his error without trying to get him to repent would be wrong and actually unkind to the man himself. Other Christian brethren are not to treat him as an enemy but to "admonish," or warn, him as a brother (II Thess. 3:15).

As we said at the beginning of the chapter, many Christians deny the idea of separating from other Christians. Both here and in I Corinthians 5 Paul clearly teaches that such separation is appropriate. Another method some use to limit such commands is to narrow their focus. Some discussions of this passage are prime examples of this approach. John R. Rice and Jack Van Impe, for instance, both argue that the passage applies only to Christians who refuse to work and have become lazy idlers, not to other forms of disobedience.[7] They are right in seeing Paul's focus on the problem of idlers. But this idleness is but one example of the willful practice of disobedience. The broader definition of "traditions" in II Thessalonians 2:15 invalidates attempts to limit the teaching of chapter 3 to one particular point of practice. Anyone who refuses to abide by any apostolic teaching (3:14) is subject to church discipline.

Old Testament Parallel

Under the Mosaic law, God required an Israelite to rebuke someone who had fallen into sin. "Thou shalt not hate thy brother in thine heart: thou shalt in any wise rebuke thy neighbour, and not suffer sin upon him" (Lev. 19:17). The Israelites who entered the Promised Land understood the principle that when some of God's people become disobedient, their brethren must first reprove and then take such action against them as might be necessary (Josh. 22:11-20). The story of the sin of Achan (Josh. 7) illustrates this principle in action as well as God's judgment on the congregation for the presence of sin. The book of Proverbs also has much to say about the principle of rebuke (e.g., 25:12; 27:5).

The situation in Israel after the return from the Babylonian captivity is a good illustration of this principle in the Old Testament. The Assyrians had brought in foreign settlers to the land after their conquest (II Kings 17:24-25; Ezra 4:2, 10). Some of the Hebrews had begun following the religious practices of the pagans and intermarried with them. The leaders of the Hebrews after the exile, Ezra and Nehemiah, confronted this situation. Ezra understood the seriousness of the sin of his brethren and the need for action (Ezra 9-10). He mourned (9:3-4) and prayed (9:5-15). Then he led the people in public penitence before God and in the putting away of the foreign wives (10:1-17). Likewise, Nehemiah recognized the importance of cleansing and disciplinary action (Neh. 13). He excluded foreigners from God's assembly (vv. 1-3), cleansed the temple (vv. 4-9), commanded the resumption of the tithe (vv. 10-14), restored the celebration of the sabbath (vv. 15-22), and commanded separation by the ending of mixed marriages (vv. 23-29).

Explanation and Application

Although many people see the necessity of separation from the world system and from teachers of false doctrine, the need for separation from a Christian brother is hard for them to accept. Ideally there should be a spiritual unity in the church, a oneness that pervades the entire body of Christ. If believers act as they should, there will be unity in the church. The church, however, does not always live up to this ideal. It has not yet been presented without spot or wrinkle, and believers are not yet all that they should be or will be. In the present everyday life of the church, therefore, it is sometimes necessary to break fellowship with a Christian brother. "It is often said that the divided condition of Christendom is an evil, and so it is," writes J. Gresham Machen. "But the evil consists in the existence of the errors which cause the divisions and not at all in the recognition of those errors when once they exist."[8]

Separation from a disobedient brother is only a part of discipline in the church. Anytime a brother is disobedient in regard to a clear command of God's Word, it becomes necessary first to rebuke him (Matt. 18:15-17; II Tim. 2:25). Matthew 18 makes it clear that if this brother fails to respond to the initial rebuke, then we must make various other efforts to correct his errant lifestyle, beliefs, or practice. Only as a last resort is it necessary to separate from this brother, and this action must not be done in a spirit of self-righteousness. With sadness, concerned Christians have to break fellowship while maintaining the hope that repentance will result. Furthermore, the act of separating from a Christian brother may vary in extent and nature from one case to another according to the severity and persistence of his disobedience.

There is a great deal of confusion concerning this kind of separation. Christians sometimes ignore it or press it beyond the guidelines set down in Scripture. It would be helpful therefore to consider some examples of situations that are likely to arise.

First, when a Christian chooses to live like the world in open sin or adopts a worldly lifestyle, he becomes a danger to other Christians. The church is obligated by Scripture to deal with him. Depending on the extent of his backsliding, he may be counseled with, excluded from positions of leadership, forbidden to take part in the public programs of the church, and even excluded from membership.

Second, if a brother becomes enamored with some teacher of a false doctrine, lends support to him, and gives him Christian recognition, then he is "partaking of his evil deeds" (II John 11). He may thereby deceive other Christians and lead them astray. The church must deal with him in much the same manner as described above.

Third, a Christian leader who refuses to take action against those who have been disobedient but instead encourages them is himself disobedient to the clear commands of the Bible. It is the responsibility of other Christian leaders to rebuke this man and eventually to separate from him if there is no repentance.

Fourth, a brother who causes divisions in the church must also come under discipline. The word *heresy* meant in New Testament times a division, and the Bible condemns schisms. The local assembly must, therefore, deal with any Christian who by his conduct or teaching disrupts the unity of the church. Ironically, some extreme separatists fall into this category by arguing for separation over minor issues of interpretation or personal differences.

Do not forget that separation from a disobedient brother is not based upon merely personal conflicts or differences of opinion on minor matters of interpretation. Denominational differences on matters of church government or mode of baptism should not preclude fellowship and cooperation with spiritual Christians of other denominations (I Cor. 1-3). Furthermore, this separation is not a total rejection that allows no place for repentance. We should make every effort to restore the brother, making full allowance for possible ignorance, errors of judgment, and momentary weakness. We should allow time for those young in the faith to achieve a degree of spiritual maturity that enables them to understand these truths. The brother who has just realized his responsibility and is moving away from compromise may be treated in a different manner from one who is abandoning a separated position and beginning to compromise the Christian faith. For example, a brother or pastor who is still in an apostate denomination but who has begun to see the problems of fellowship with these people should be taught and encouraged to make a complete break with his past associations.

We cannot stress too strongly that separation from another Christian is not the same as separation from an apostate teacher. In both cases, purity is a goal. However, in separation from a Christian, restoration is also a goal. We may hope that separation from a false teacher might be a means of reaching him with the truth (II Tim. 2:24-25), but we are commanded to remember that erring Christians are our brothers and need to be restored to a harmonious family relationship. "If we lump our [disobedient] brothers together with apostates under the general heading of 'ecclesiastical separation,' it isn't long before we are speaking of and treating our brothers as though they were apostates."[9]

Exactly how do we practice separation in everyday life? The Amish practice what is known as "shunning." When the Amish exclude someone from their church, they forbid all communication with him. Even a wife whose husband is shunned is not to eat with him or she will be excluded too. Shunning, however, is far more extreme than the Bible's teaching concerning separation. As a general principle, Christians should not indulge in any activity that gives apparent approval to a person's wrongdoing.

A Christian whose sin is not publicly known and who is not leading others astray by his example should be rebuked privately. While a stronger brother should try to rebuke and, if possible, restore a weaker brother, he should do it in a spirit of meekness, remembering that he may also be tempted. However, public sin committed by a public figure must be publicly rebuked for the sake of those who are being deceived. For example, a man who advocates fellowship with apostasy and who cooperates with false teachers and unbelievers is guilty of a public defiance of God's command. For the sake of those whom he is leading astray or who might be led astray by him if not properly warned from the Scripture, a faithful minister of Christ must warn against that man even though he pretends to, and perhaps to an extent does, preach the gospel. At best, this is a situation in which a disobedient Christian is behaving like a false teacher. It is unfortunate that men are associated with positions. It would be well if we could concentrate only on the position and deal with the issue of scriptural disobedience or compromise. But when some man is the prime instigator, promoter, and advocate of an unbiblical position, we must expose that man as we denounce the sin he is promoting.

As with other forms of separation, there are Christians who object to separating from disobedient Christians. One argument is that separation from other Christians can be only on moral grounds. Donald Grey Barnhouse insists, "There must be separation where there is *moral* lapse, but *there is never a hint of separation because of doctrinal differences.*"[10] Barnhouse even offered $100 to anyone who could cite a single verse in the Bible justifying separation from a Christian on doctrinal grounds.[11] Walter Martin joins him in contending that separation can be only on moral grounds unless the doctrinal error is causing divisions in the church.[12] We mentioned earlier that the reference to idolatry in I Corinthians 5:11 weighs against this view, for certainly idolatry is a doctrinal error.[13] But more than that, this argument misses the central point of separation. We do not simply itemize all the sins specifically mentioned in Scripture and say, "These are the only grounds for separation." Rather, we affirm the principle that the willful, unrepentant practice of any sin is a cause for separation because all such sin is an affront to the holiness of God.

As we mentioned in Chapter 1, some Christians speak of first-degree and second-degree (or primary and secondary) separation.

By first-degree separation they mean separation from those who teach false doctrine. Second-degree separation involves separation from those believers who do not practice first-degree separation. Some Christians ridicule the position of second-degree separation as unscriptural, saying that it will lead to extremes.[14] Robert Lightner asks, "What about what has been called second-degree separation or third-, fourth-, or even fifth-degree separation? Are God's people to separate from others of God's people who do not separate? How far removed from the original offender should one carry the matter of separation? Specific answers to these questions are not given in the Bible."[15]

As we have shown, however, faithfulness to biblical principles sometimes makes separation from other believers necessary. Although some staunch separatists have used this language, this kind of separation really should not be called "secondary" but *biblical* separation. "There is no such thing as first-degree separation, second-degree separation, and so forth. There is only Scriptural separation."[16] Paul illustrates this point in the warnings in II Thessalonians 3. There Paul commands believers to have "no company with" the disobedient brother. Had the Thessalonians refused, they would not have been guilty simply of associating with someone who was disobedient. They would have been themselves guilty of disobedience in refusing to heed Paul's command.

In addition to underestimating the seriousness of disobedience, those condemning "secondary" separation miss the Bible's warnings concerning the contaminating effects of associating with disobedience. Citing I Corinthians 15:33, Rolland McCune observes, "While some may debate whether or not there is a legitimate 'condemnation by association,' there is certainly a genuine 'corruption by association' that takes place in wrong alliances."[17] It is not a question of separating from those who do not separate; it is a matter of separating from sin, from a willful disobedience to what God commands.

Purposes

Concerned Christians separate from disobedient brethren, therefore, for the following reasons:

1. To preserve the testimony of God's people in the eyes of the world (I Pet. 2:12).

2. To prevent a disobedient brother from influencing others to do wrong (I Cor. 5:6-7; Gal. 5:9).

3. To set an example which will encourage others to be obedient (I Tim. 5:20).

4. To bring about repentance in the one who has been disobedient (II Tim. 2:25; Rev. 3:19).

We may at first be perplexed when we try to think of separation from disobedient Christians in terms of Christlikeness. We know that Jesus invites the sinner to Himself and says, "Come unto me, all ye that labour and are heavy laden, and I will give you rest" (Matt. 11:28). But we have already mentioned that Christ's purpose is to save and cleanse His church as a bride for Himself (Eph. 5:25-27). Christ Himself gave the first teaching concerning church discipline (Matt. 18:15-18). Those He loves, Christ says, He rebukes and chastens that they might repent (Rev. 3:19). We can also say this much as a caution: any church discipline or form of separation that is undertaken without a concern for love and holiness is not a Christlike practice.

Conclusion

As we look back on Chapters 3-5, there are some important general conclusions we should keep in mind concerning the practice of biblical separation. First, in separation, as in other aspects of Christian living, believers must act according to the principle of love. But Christian love is not weak sentimentality; "biblical love is to be informed, discerning, and discriminating (Phil. 1:9-10)."[18] True biblical separation is manifested in love: a love for God that rejects the world system, a love for the church that will not tolerate false teachers who desire to lead the sheep astray and to devour them, and a love for the Christian brother that is willing to endure even a break in fellowship in order to provoke him to do right. In the practice of separation, Christians should not become frustrated or vindictive. They should not be hasty to condemn others on the basis of unproven rumors. Instead they should demonstrate a godly patience because they know that God will eventually judge all ungodliness (Jude 14-15), whether it be the ungodliness of the world, of the false teacher, or of a disobedient brother.

Second, many who argue against scriptural separation as presented here are not against separation as a principle. They will separate from other believers because of disagreements over minor matters of interpretation or practice that do not involve the fundamentals of the Faith. But they have an unbalanced view of the Scripture and fail to see the seriousness of the sin that makes separation absolutely necessary. The believer who immerses himself in the Word of God and seeks to mature spiritually must learn to view sin the way God does.

Third, there is always the danger of extremism in separation. Personal interpretations are elevated to points of division, and separation is practiced almost for its own sake rather than out of sound biblical conviction. "Separation is God's answer to apostasy. Separation is God's answer to the problem of disobedient brethren who will not separate from apostasy. But, separation is not the answer to every disagreement between brethren."[19]

In summary, believers practicing biblical separation will avoid individuals who are evil in conduct, false in teaching, and unspiritual in lifestyle. They should do so to the glory of God and to conform themselves to the image of Jesus Christ.

Fundamentalism
Chapter 6

The concept of biblical separation is closely identified with Fundamentalism. Indeed, it is so identified with the movement that we have spent five chapters laying out the biblical basis of separation to correct the misconception that separation is nothing more than the practice of some contemporary "ism."

Since the 1970s, there has been a steady stream of books and articles studying American Fundamentalism.[1] Some of these have been extremely helpful, and others have been rather less so. In a single chapter we can only survey the history and beliefs of Fundamentalism. We recommend you look at the notes for guidance on some particular point. We will focus on the definition of Fundamentalism, briefly survey the history of the movement, and discuss some general considerations necessary for understanding the nature of Fundamentalism.

Because our topic is biblical separation, we will look particularly at how Fundamentalism has taught and practiced separation. You will see how the principles we studied in previous chapters have actually been applied. You will also see that the principle of separation has been applied in different manners, including both the expulsion of false teaching and the withdrawal from it. Above all, you will see that, practically speaking, Fundamentalism today represents the fullest expression of the practice of the principles of biblical separation that we have been discussing.

Defining Fundamentalism

Sometimes Fundamentalism is dismissed as nothing more than a reaction to religious liberalism. Truly, it has been shaped by its opposition to liberalism, but that characteristic cannot explain the whole movement. More recently, you may have heard the term *fundamentalist* used with non-Christian traditionalist religious groups. Islamic terrorists killing villagers in Algeria are called "Muslim fundamentalists," or members of a Jewish group planning to bomb a Muslim mosque in Jerusalem are called "Jewish fundamentalists." This definition is based on supposed similarities between these movements and Christian Fundamentalism. In fact, this is probably (and unfortunately) the most popular scholarly approach to the study of Fundamentalism today. The way certain groups practice their beliefs and the way they hold those beliefs is allegedly what makes them "fundamentalist." This approach mocks the content of those beliefs, though. Christians who insist on the truth of the Trinity, for example, are placed in the same category with Muslims and Jews who think the doctrine of the Trinity is heresy. What you believe, this approach argues, is irrelevant compared to how you believe it, at least as far as being a "fundamentalist" is concerned.[2]

A true definition of Fundamentalism will take into account what Fundamentalists believe as well as how they practice their beliefs. Here is the basic definition we will use: Fundamentalism is the belief (1) that there are certain truths so essential to Christianity that they cannot be denied without destroying Christianity and (2) that these essentials are the basis of Christian fellowship. The first point is the distinction between Fundamentalism on the one hand and liberalism, Neo-orthodoxy, and Roman Catholicism (discussed in Chapters 7, 8, and 11) on the other. The second point is the distinction between Fundamentalism on one side and the New Evangelicalism and the Charismatic movement (discussed in Chapters 9 and 10) on the other. In terms of our theme of separation, the first point involves the Bible's teaching concerning separation from false teachers, and the second point involves separation from disobedient Christians.

There are also some historical characteristics of the movement that are not covered by this definition but which we should note. At least three features also characterize Fundamentalism as it is commonly practiced. These features are theological development, cultural factors, and historical continuity.

Fundamentalism has reaped the benefit from centuries of development in Christian theology, but this idea of theological development requires some explanation. The truth of God is eternal and unchanging; truth does not develop, and we do not invent it. But the Bible is not a systematic book of theology. Throughout church history we have seen the church grapple with important questions and, as a result, study the Scripture for answers to those questions. The doctrine of the Trinity is a good example. Until Arius actively denied Christ's deity in the fourth century, Christians had never set down the Bible's teaching concerning that doctrine in systematic fashion. The challenge of Arius, however, led to the Councils of Nicea (325) and Constantinople (381). These councils wrote creeds that summarized the biblical teaching concerning Christ.[3]

Likewise, Fundamentalism has seen theological development in stating biblical teaching. Dispensationalism, as we will see, was important to the development of Fundamentalism. Clearly, it was a new system in the nineteenth century, but that fact does not necessarily weigh against the scriptural validity of its beliefs. The inerrancy of Scripture was far from a new doctrine, but it certainly took on a new importance in the face of liberalism. Some writers try to argue that Fundamentalism either "invented" inerrancy or at least made inerrancy more important than it had traditionally been in Christian teaching. Inerrancy has clearly been a historic teaching of the Christian faith,[4] but like many teachings of Scripture in history, inerrancy was emphasized most when it came under attack. The liberal attack on the authority of Scripture naturally caused conservatives to stress the biblical teaching of inerrancy more than it had been stressed in the past.[5]

Cultural factors also characterize Fundamentalism. It is sometimes difficult for Christians to distinguish which of their views are scriptural and which are the result of their cultural heritage. Hudson Taylor shocked his fellow missionaries in the 1800s by abandoning Western ways to live and dress like the Chinese people he wished to reach with the gospel. One prominent cultural factor among Fundamentalists was viewing American culture as the height of Christian civilization. William Jennings Bryan is an example of this tendency. He opposed evolution partly because he saw it as an enemy of America's Christian civilization.[6] The United States has a rich Christian heritage, but the nation has never been perfect, as shown by ugly episodes in its past such as slavery, racial prejudice, and the treatment of the Indians. Our model for Christianity is to be found in the Bible, not in the history of any nation.

Unfortunately, some writers have tried to define Fundamentalism entirely by its cultural features. Historians of a feminist bent, for instance, have defined Fundamentalism as primarily a reaction to changing gender roles in America. Some of their observations are valid, but their conclusions are not. It is true that Fundamentalists reflect their culture; everyone does. It is quite another thing to say that the real root of Fundamentalism is found in these factors. To argue that culture is the determining factor is to ignore much evidence to the contrary.[7]

It is important that we balance theological development and cultural factors with the important truth of historical continuity. Orthodox Christians of the past did not share all the characteristics of Fundamentalism. But the movement shares in the orthodox theology of historic Christianity. Liberal Kirsopp Lake of Harvard made an observation about Fundamentalism in 1925 that has been often cited:

> But it is a mistake, often made by educated persons who happen to have but little knowledge of historical theology, to suppose that Fundamentalism is a new and strange form of thought. It is nothing of the kind: it is the partial and uneducated survival of a theology which was once universally held by all Christians. How many were there, for instance, in Christian churches in the eighteenth century who doubted the infallible inspiration of all Scripture? A few, perhaps, but very few. No, the Fundamentalist may be wrong; I think that he is. But it is we who have departed from the tradition, not he, and I am sorry for the fate of anyone who tries to argue with a Fundamentalist on the basis of authority. The Bible and the *corpus theologicum* [doctrinal body] of the Church is [*sic*] on the Fundamentalist side.[8]

Christians of past ages may not have been "Fundamentalists," but if somehow such Christians could look at the points on which Fundamentalists and liberals differ, it is hard to imagine them not preferring the Fundamentalist side. The movements that gave rise to Fundamentalism did not agree with each other entirely on all points of interpretation, but they shared a common commitment to historic Christian orthodoxy.

Although Fundamentalism is a contemporary movement with contemporary features, it is a movement expressing the historic Christian faith. Fundamentalists affirm the teachings of the creeds of the early church councils concerning the Trinity, Christ's deity, His divine and human natures, and other biblical doctrines. They claim the doctrines held in common by the great Reformation confessions concerning the nature of salvation, the sufficiency of Scripture, and other teachings the reformers proclaimed in opposition to Catholic error. Whatever its other features, at the heart of Fundamentalism lies "the faith which was once delivered unto the saints."

A Brief History of Fundamentalism

We will divide the history of Fundamentalism into four periods. Such an approach is always a little artificial because historical movements do not actually break into neat periods. But each of these periods represents clear developments in the history of Fundamentalism and its practice of separation.

Formation of the Fundamentalist Coalition (1865-1919)

There is no date for the official founding of Fundamentalism. A number of movements—each with its own origins and influenced by a number of different factors—came together in response to liberalism to form what we know as Fundamentalism. Actually the term *Fundamentalist* was not coined until after this period. Also some Christians involved in the movements that contributed to the rise of Fundamentalism later distanced themselves from Fundamentalism itself. Yet these movements contributed the ideas and institutions that shaped Fundamentalism and inspired many of the leaders who guided it.

This joining of movements came after the American Civil War. Until that time Evangelical Protestantism had dominated American culture. Although the United States had no established state church under the First Amendment, Protestantism was almost unofficially established. Virtually all colleges, for example, were church-related and had clergymen as their presidents. Catholics considered the public schools so Protestant that they often formed their own parochial schools to protect their children from Protestant influence.

This interdenominational Protestantism expressed its dominance through cooperative efforts. Bible societies, mission agencies, and movements for social reform (e.g., the abolition of slavery, the prohibition of the sale of alcohol) were often interdenominational efforts. One facet of Evangelical Protestantism that Fundamentalists later treasured was the nation's heritage of revivals and evangelism. The Prayer Meeting Revival of 1857-59 contributed directly to the movements that gave rise to Fundamentalism, such as Bible conferences. The great expression of revival and evangelism after the Civil War was found in the citywide campaigns of evangelists such as D. L. Moody. Later Billy Sunday and other prominent evangelists became major leaders in Fundamentalism.[9]

This dominance began to break up in the late 1800s. Immigration of non-Protestants began to increase, reducing Protestantism's numerical advantage. Intellectual movements challenged the Christian faith. Charles Darwin's *Origin of Species* laid the foundation for the theory of biological evolution, and in so doing called the authority of Scripture into question. Other intellectual movements appeared to undermine Christianity. Reason and particularly science were widely assumed to be the roads to truth. If Christianity clashed with science and reason, critics implied, then so much the worse for Christianity.

The invasion of this spirit of science and rationalism into the church really sparked the formation of Fundamentalism. Liberalism, called *Modernism* in the late 1800s and early 1900s, represented that spirit. (We will look more fully at the development of liberalism in the next chapter.) Ironically, Modernists were not as extreme as some secular rationalists. The Modernists agreed that Protestantism should dominate American culture. They wanted to maintain that dominance, however, by changing Christianity to suit the temper of the times. They would modernize the faith to appeal to modern man. "Modernizing" the faith, unfortunately, meant abandoning the inerrancy and authority of the Scripture and questioning such teachings as Christ's deity, His miracles, and His physical resurrection from the dead.[10]

A whole coalition of conservatives began to resist Modernism, but many of these movements already existed. Opposition to Modernism simply united them. For example, one rising force in nineteenth-century American Christianity was premillennialism. There have been premillennialists throughout history, but they became influential in American religion only after the Civil War. Most American Christians until that time were postmillennialists. They believed that the Holy Spirit would work through the church until the gospel spread throughout the world. When the world had been brought to Christ, then Jesus Himself would return for the final judgment.

Premillennialists, on the other hand, believed that there would be a great outpouring of God's wrath upon the earth followed by Christ's return to establish a millennial (thousand-year) kingdom. Premillennialists were especially opposed to the Modernist perversion of postmillennialism. Modernists argued that mankind would build a perfect world through teaching and practicing Christian principles. They did not believe, as the conservative postmillennialists did, in the person and work of the Holy Spirit or the literal return of Christ.[11]

Premillennial teaching was popularized through books, tracts, and religious newspapers. Two new vehicles for promoting premillennialism were Bible conferences and Bible training schools. At Bible conferences, Christians gathered at vacation spots to hear concentrated Bible teaching from leading ministers and teachers. At such conferences listeners took in orthodox Bible teaching and returned home to spread the teaching further. One of the most important conferences was the Niagara Bible Conference in the late 1800s led by James H. Brookes. This conference was not only a center of premillennial teaching but also a rallying point for those who affirmed the essential doctrines of Christianity that Modernism was denying. The creed of this conference, adopted in 1878, is often considered the first creed of the Fundamentalist movement.[12]

Some Christians also began to form Bible training schools. As their name suggests, these schools concentrated mostly on education in the Bible and practical topics such as personal evangelism and Sunday school work. Their goal was to train lay workers or sometimes ministers and missionaries for Christian work. Their curriculum was based on theologically conservative study of the English Bible with usually a heavy stress on premillennialism. Many of the early Bible schools were Bible institutes. They did not offer a full college program but only a Bible-study program with perhaps a few courses in English or speech. The most famous institute was founded by D. L. Moody in Chicago; after his death it was renamed Moody Bible Institute. Later, many Bible institutes adopted full collegiate programs and became Bible colleges, Christian liberal arts colleges, and seminaries.[13]

These publications, conferences, and schools sometimes taught different forms of premillennialism. The most important form for the formation of Fundamentalism was dispensationalism. This system is named for the different ages, or *dispensations,* it sees in history. In each of these dispensations, God tests mankind in some way, and each age ends with man's failure and God's judgment. Central to dispensationalism is a distinction between Israel and the church. Certain parts of the Bible, including a great deal of prophecy, apply only to the Jews, and other parts apply only to Christians. Dispensationalists stressed teachings that later characterized Fundamentalism in general: the inerrancy of Scripture; the falling away of most of Christendom from the truth before the return of Christ; and the Rapture, the coming of Christ for His church just before God's wrath is poured out on earth. J. N. Darby of the Plymouth Brethren in Britain is usually considered the founder of dispensationalism.

The system was popularized in America by Congregationalist minister C. I. Scofield. His Scofield Reference Bible (first edition 1909) exposed millions of Christians to dispensationalist teaching.[14]

Another influence was Keswick holiness teaching. (The Methodist form of holiness teaching had less influence on Fundamentalism than the Keswick kind.) Named for a conference site in England, the Keswick approach stressed the need for personal holiness through the power of the Holy Spirit. Although not accepting all Keswick teachings, many Fundamentalists embraced some ideas such as the "victorious" or "abundant life" and the existence of two distinct natures in the believer (a corrupt old nature and a regenerate new nature). Particularly popular was the idea of a special experience following conversion, often called "surrender," in which a Christian moves to a higher level of spiritual development and maturity.[15]

Modernism was initially a movement of scholars. Among its opponents therefore were orthodox scholars, who responded to its teachings. The main center of orthodox scholarship was Princeton Theological Seminary, which stood firmly against liberalism and upheld the inerrancy of the Bible. Princeton's Benjamin B. Warfield was probably the leading scholarly defender of inerrancy at the turn of the twentieth century. The Princeton men were not concerned with just inerrancy, however. They realized that Modernism was cutting out the heart of Christianity as a redemptive religion, and they opposed the movement's errors on a range of issues. Warfield died in 1921, but the cause of the Princeton theology in the Fundamentalist-Modernist controversy was carried on by J. Gresham Machen.[16]

Each of these movements opposed aspects of Modernism and contributed to the rise of Fundamentalism. The blending of these movements is seen in the publication of a series of pamphlets called *The Fundamentals* (1910-15).[17] Sponsored by two Christian businessmen, these twelve pamphlets contained articles written by the best orthodox scholars of the day, men such as Warfield and Scofield. The articles defended the inspiration and authority of the

Bible, attacked evolution, and defended the biblical teaching concerning Christ. The sponsors mailed thousands of these pamphlets at no cost to pastors, missionaries, and laymen. The pamphlets were, as their subtitle said, "A Testimony to the Truth." In a few years this idea of defending the fundamentals would develop into the term *Fundamentalism.*

In this period, expulsion more than withdrawal was the usual pattern of separation. An exception was Oliver Van Osdel of the Wealthy Street Baptist Church in Grand Rapids. He led his church out of the Northern Baptist Convention in 1909. Since conservatives for the most part controlled the major denominations, they took steps to eliminate error. In 1910 the Presbyterian Church in the USA began requiring candidates for the ministry to affirm their belief in five essential doctrines: the inerrancy of the Bible, the virgin birth of Christ, His vicarious atonement, His bodily resurrection, and the genuineness of biblical miracles. Furthermore, Presbyterians conducted heresy trials of liberal theologians and ministers in an attempt to put them out of the church.[18]

Fundamentalist-Modernist Controversy (1919-36)

Most people who know at least a little about Fundamentalism will often associate it with what is known as the Fundamentalist-Modernist controversy in the 1920s. Modernists and Fundamentalists clashed over who would control the major denominations and their agencies (schools, mission boards, publishing houses).[19]

A prelude to the controversy was the founding of the World's Christian Fundamentals Association (WCFA) in 1919 under the presidency of Minnesota Baptist W. B. Riley. The WCFA represented the first major attempt to unite conservatives and coordinate their efforts against Modernism.[20] The following year Baptist editor Curtis Lee Laws coined a name for this movement when he wrote, "We suggest that those who still cling to the great fundamentals and who mean to do battle royal for the fundamentals shall be called 'Fundamentalists.' "[21]

The major battles took place in the Northern Baptist Convention (NBC) and the Presbyterian Church in the USA (PCUSA). The

Fundamentalists tried to exclude Modernism from their denominations; Modernists attempted to make the denominations include all shades of theological belief. The Fundamentalist slogan was "Truth," and the Modernist slogan was "Tolerance."

Fundamentalists in the NBC began organizing in 1920, founding the Fundamentalist Fellowship to lobby for orthodoxy. The climax was an effort in 1922 to adopt a creed and thereby force the Modernists out. The Modernists offered a counterproposal affirming "that the New Testament is the all-sufficient ground of our faith and practice, and we need no other statement."[22] The New Testament won the vote hands down. Although skirmishing continued for several years, the NBC rejected the Fundamentalist position and committed itself to tolerating theological diversity.[23]

Another effort among Baptists was the Baptist Bible Union (BBU), founded in 1923. This organization attempted to rally all Baptists for the Fundamentalist cause in their respective denominations. W. B. Riley in the North, J. Frank Norris of Texas in the South, and T. T. Shields in Canada were the main leaders. The BBU foundered, however, especially after two public-relations disasters. Thinking his life was in danger, Norris shot a man in his office in 1926. Although he was acquitted of murder, Norris's reputation was seriously damaged. In 1927 Shields led a BBU attempt to transform a liberal NBC school, Des Moines University, into a Fundamentalist institution. The student body resented the effort, rioted, and forced the closing of the school in 1929. These disasters wrecked the BBU almost beyond repair.[24]

In the Presbyterian Church the major Fundamentalist leader was J. Gresham Machen of Princeton Seminary. He wrote the most important Fundamentalist apologetic, *Christianity and Liberalism* (1923), arguing that Modernism was not even Christian. However, an alliance of liberals and tolerant conservatives in the PCUSA attacked the denomination's five-point doctrinal test for ministers. When that test finally was overturned in 1927, the denomination then reorganized Princeton Seminary to remove it from conservative control. Machen and several others left Princeton to found Westminster Theological Seminary. Then Machen protested liberalism among the denomination's missionaries by founding an independent mission board in 1933. The Presbyterians tried Machen for violating church discipline and suspended him. He then formed a new denomination in 1936 that eventually became known as the Orthodox Presbyterian Church. The Fundamentalists had lost almost all the denominational battles among both the Baptists and the Presbyterians.[25]

One other aspect of the Fundamentalist-Modernist controversy was the crusade against evolution in the South. Christians sought legislation to forbid the teaching of evolution in public schools. This movement climaxed with the Scopes Trial in Dayton, Tennessee, in 1925. A local schoolteacher, John Scopes, was tried for violating Tennessee's anti-evolution law. Scopes was defended by agnostic attorney Clarence Darrow, supported by the American Civil Liberties Union. Leading the prosecution was statesman and Presbyterian Fundamentalist William Jennings Bryan. The devout Bryan opposed evolution in part because it conflicted with the Bible's account of Creation. But, as we mentioned earlier, he also attacked evolution because he said it was a cruel philosophy of life that would destroy what Bryan saw as Christian civilization as it existed in the United States. Scopes was convicted, but Fundamentalism was made to look ridiculous in the media. The Scopes Trial was seen as yet another defeat.[26]

There was much more going on in this period beside these battles. We should note, however, how separation was being expressed at this time. There was first an attempt to cleanse the denominations and their institutions. Failure of that effort led to a partial withdrawal and the widespread establishment of independent Fundamentalist institutions. Resistance to Modernism remained, but it began to take a different form.

Independent Fundamentalism (1925-57)

You will notice that this period overlaps the Fundamentalist-Modernist controversy. As the controversy was going on, Fundamentalists gradually realized that the battle was going against them. Therefore they began to build their own network of schools, publishing houses, mission boards, and eventually denominations. If they could not clean up the denominational institutions, then they would found their own.[27]

There are many examples of this trend. We have already mentioned how Machen founded the Orthodox Presbyterian Church. The remnant of the Bible Baptist Union re-formed itself into the General Association of Regular Baptist Churches in 1932. Other Fundamentalists left the Northern Baptist Convention in 1947 and formed the Conservative Baptist Association. Fundamentalists continued to rely on the Bible schools founded before the controversy, such as Moody Bible Institute, Biola, and Wheaton College. New schools included Dallas Theological Seminary, a center of dispensationalist teaching (founded 1924), and Bob Jones College (1927), later Bob Jones University. Fundamentalist mission boards grew and began to surpass the boards of the major denominations in sending missionaries to the field. Bible conferences continued to function as centers for spreading orthodox theology and to provide opportunities for fellowship among Fundamentalists.

Fundamentalists also made use of mass media. They continued to publish periodicals and religious newspapers, such as *The Sunday School Times* and John R. Rice's *Sword of the Lord* (founded 1934). Radio became a popular vehicle for promoting the Fundamentalist cause. One of the most successful broadcasters was Charles Fuller. His "Old-Fashioned Revival Hour" became one of the most popular religious radio programs in America during the 1930s and 1940s.

There was an irony in all of this activity. Fundamentalists and Modernists had battled to see which would control the major denominations. One assumption was that whoever won would then superintend Protestantism's historic dominance in American culture. The Modernists and their conservative allies gained control and established a policy of tolerance. For several years, the major denominations maintained their position and then began in the 1960s to suffer a precipitous decline in membership. Meanwhile, the Fundamentalists on the fringes of American life began to flourish. Their organizations grew and thrived so that by the 1950s and 1960s some religious observers began to refer to Fundamentalism/Evangelicalism as a "third force" in American religion alongside Catholicism and mainstream Protestantism.[28]

The word *independent* describes Fundamentalism in this period. Fundamentalism remained opposed to liberalism and was separatist in refusing to cooperate with liberalism, hence the many independent agencies. But Fundamentalists did not always agree about breaking all official ties to liberalism. Ernest Pickering has rightly pointed out how the General Association of Regular Baptist Churches (GARBC) and the Conservative Baptist Association (CBA) represented differing philosophies. The GARBC from its founding did not allow its churches to hold membership in organizations such as the Northern Baptist Convention, which contained Modernists. The CBA allowed its members to hold dual membership in its body as well as groups such as the Northern Baptists.[29] What is sometimes missed, however, is that both the GARBC and the CBA were initially considered Fundamentalist.

Fundamentalists agreed that they should not support liberalism. The question was what was meant by "support." Was the kind of association practiced by the CBA a form of support? In the 1950s this question of the Christian's precise relations to liberalism became the focus of a new controversy. But regardless of official connections, Fundamentalists in this period were independent in mind. They rejected the teachings of liberalism and focused their energy and fellowship on their own orthodox organizations.

Separatist Fundamentalism (1957 to the Present)

The use of the word *separatist* for this period does not mean that Fundamentalism was not separatist before this time. As we have argued, there has always been an implied division that was expressed not only as withdrawal but also expulsion and the building of independent organizations. The events of this period, however, brought the question of separatist withdrawal to the front.

Just as we need to look at liberalism in Chapter 7 before we can fully understand the Fundamentalist-Modernist controversy, so we need to look at Chapter 9 on the New Evangelicalism to fully understand separatist Fundamentalism. For now, let us just preview the New Evangelical movement so that we can understand the Fundamentalist reaction. In the 1940s and 1950s, a number of Evangelical scholars and spokesmen began calling for the reform of Fundamentalism. They wished to see greater Evangelical involvement in scholarship through discussion of theological issues with liberals. They also repudiated the idea of separation and called for infiltration back into the major denominations to recapture them.

The man who became the symbol of this movement and whose actions marked this division was not a scholar, however, but an evangelist. Billy Graham, probably the best-known Evangelical preacher in America, embraced the New Evangelical cause. The break between New Evangelicals and Fundamentalists really became final in 1957 when Graham announced, "I would like to make myself quite clear. I intend to go anywhere, sponsored by anybody, to preach the Gospel of Christ, if there are no strings attached to my message."[30] In his New York campaign of that year, he accepted liberal sponsors on his committee, and he sent converts from his campaign into liberal churches.

A large group of Fundamentalists denounced this action as a betrayal of what they had been fighting for since the 1920s. In 1958 a group of more than 150 Fundamentalist leaders met in Chicago to respond to Graham. Led by Bob Jones Sr. of Bob Jones University and John R. Rice of *The Sword of the Lord,* the attenders pledged to have no fellowship or other religious connection with liberalism. Among the signers were Robert Ketcham, major leader of the GARBC; G. B. Vick, major leader of the Baptist Bible Fellowship; and Jack Hyles, a leading independent Baptist.[31] Graham's action, the pledge implied, was not some vague question of associations; it was a conscious embrace of liberals.

The result of Graham's action was to make separatism a major issue. Graham's alliances with liberals caused Fundamentalists to look closely at the dangers of even casual religious ties to liberals. They would no longer be vague about what constituted "support" of liberalism. They insisted on breaking all links so that there was no question of association.

Conservative Protestantism soon divided into two camps. Some who did not consider themselves "New" Evangelicals still supported Graham because of his extensive, apparently successful evangelistic work. Those who opposed Graham's methodology, and the New Evangelical philosophy it represented, kept the name *Fundamentalist.* As we will discuss more fully in Chapter 9, the initial disagreement between these two factions was not on an essential point of doctrine (as it had been with the liberals) but on the matter of biblical separation itself.

The ramifications of this division were felt throughout American Evangelicalism. Some groups, such as the GARBC, came down solidly on the Fundamentalist side, but many split. The Conservative Baptist Association, as we mentioned, had allowed its members to maintain some ties to organizations that tolerated liberalism. The majority of the CBA sided with the New Evangelical policy in maintaining such associations. A sizeable minority, however, left the CBA to pursue a Fundamentalist policy of excluding all ties to liberalism.[32]

The history of Fundamentalism since the late 1950s has been far from uneventful, but space limits how much we can mention.[33] The movement has become more predominantly Baptist in this period,[34] but there are still significant numbers of nondenominational Fundamentalists and Fundamentalist remnants among the Presbyterians, Methodists, and other groups. A major controversy in the 1970s and 1980s was over what is sometimes called "Neo-Fundamentalism"; this clash is discussed in Chapter 9. Other issues confronting the movement have included the Charismatic movement, Calvinism, and the use of the King James Version of the Bible.[35] Despite a sometimes contentious history, some four million Americans still identify themselves as Fundamentalists.[36]

Cautions on Using History

One point that we have stressed is that Scripture, not history, sets the pattern of how we should believe and live. The same truth applies to the history of Fundamentalism. Although it is helpful to draw models from history, you should not determine your attitude toward separation by appealing to a Fundamentalist practice of the past. Some New Evangelicals appeal to the pattern set in the early period of Fundamentalism. Millard Erickson cites the example of *The Fundamentals* as a model: adherence to the fundamentals of the Faith, a scholarly defense of the truth, and an alleged openness on questions such as inerrancy and evolution. Erickson contends that "the new evangelicals appear to be closer to the fundamentalism of 1910 than were the later fundamentalists."[37] Likewise, Robert L. Sumner accuses David Beale of "changing the rules in the middle of the game" by arguing that after 1930 Fundamentalists began to practice separation in a different manner in the light of a different situation.[38] The Bible is our guide for faith and practice. The study of history may help us in our study of the Bible, but it is the Scripture alone that controls our conduct.

Understanding Fundamentalism

There are still some characteristics of and questions concerning the Fundamentalist movement that we should consider. We want to answer the charge that Fundamentalism reduces theology to a "lowest common denominator" and to look at what is truly meant by Fundamentalist "militancy." Also, we wish to acknowledge the testimony of other separatists who do not consider themselves part of the Fundamentalist movement and discover why they refuse this identification.

Fundamentalism's "Reduction" of Theology

Some critics charge that Fundamentalists reduce Christianity to just a few doctrines. Harold O. J. Brown, for example, says that Protestant orthodoxy "is doctrinally comprehensive, while fundamentalism is highly selective"; orthodoxy "presents a broad range of doctrines it considers vital, and integrates them into a dogmatic system" whereas Fundamentalism "selects a small number of doctrines as fundamental and fights for them."[39]

This charge misunderstands the nature of Fundamentalism. Broadly speaking, the movement holds to the beliefs of orthodox Protestantism. Specifically, the movement insists that there are essentials of Christian belief apart from which Christianity cannot exist. Fundamentalism does not argue that these essentials are the whole of Christian doctrine. In fact, these essentials are generally those challenged by liberalism. Were Fundamentalism confronting Roman Catholicism, then doctrines such as justification by faith alone and the sole mediatorship of Christ would become prominent. Fundamentalism aims to unite believers in defense of the Faith despite their differences. Christians may hold to competing systems of theology (dispensationalism, Calvinism, Arminianism) and yet still be united in Fundamentalist testimony to the truths of Christianity. No one need deny his theological heritage or system of theology in order to be a Fundamentalist. Indeed, we must ask Brown, which system of Protestant orthodoxy should all Christians adopt?

Fundamentalist Militancy

Another common misunderstanding is the idea of "militancy" or "militant Fundamentalism." Common synonyms for *militant* include *combative, belligerent, contentious, extreme, pugnacious,* and *disputatious.* Ronald Nash castigates Fundamentalism on this basis: "One of the prime 'virtues' of the twentieth-century separatist is theological pugnaciousness. One can hear them speak proudly and boastfully of their 'militant fundamentalism,' 'uncompromising fundamentalism,' 'fighting fundamentalism,' and so on, *ad nauseam.*"[40] Furthermore, those who speak of "Muslim fundamentalism" or "Jewish fundamentalism" base their argument on the claim that being militant about your faith (whatever that faith may be) is what makes you a "fundamentalist."

There is a standard theological use of the world *militant,* however, that explains the meaning of the phrase "militant Fundamentalism." Christians have historically used the phrases "the church militant" and "the church triumphant." The church triumphant consists of the redeemed who are in heaven enjoying the presence of God. The church militant is the church upon earth engaged in warfare against sin. It is in this sense—warfare against sin—that the Fundamentalist is "militant." Paul uses this imagery, telling the Ephesians to put on a spiritual soldier's equipment, "the whole armour of God" (Eph. 6:10-17). He urges Timothy to "endure hardness, as a good soldier of Jesus Christ" and warns that "no man that warreth entangleth himself with the affairs of this life; that he may please him who hath chosen him to be a soldier" (II Tim. 2:3-4; see also I Tim. 6:12; II Tim. 4:7).

Because they truly believe in the Christian faith, Fundamentalists defend that faith. The idea of basing Christian fellowship on the fundamentals assumes militancy, making commitment to the cause the basis of all alliances. Fundamentalism starts with theological belief, and the "militant" form of behavior results. But militancy can be no excuse for sin. As Moritz notes, Fundamentalists must be militant, but they must also manifest the fruit of the Spirit.[41] A "good soldier of Jesus Christ" is not a plundering soldier of fortune but a servant who obeys his commander in all things.

Other Separatists

Finally, we must acknowledge that there are others who are in some sense separatists but who are not Fundamentalists. It is too easy for Fundamentalists in their concern about separation to become like Elijah in the wilderness. In the midst of despair, the prophet told God, "The children of Israel have forsaken thy covenant, thrown down thine altars, and slain thy prophets with the sword; and I, even I only, am left" (I Kings 19:14). But God replied to Elijah, "I have left me seven thousand in Israel, all the knees which have not bowed unto Baal, and every mouth which hath not kissed him" (v. 18).

We have mentioned already the testimonies of Charles Spurgeon and D. Martyn Lloyd-Jones. Before Fundamentalism ever arose in America, Spurgeon condemned the rise of liberalism in Britain's Baptist Union. When that group determined to tolerate unbelief, Spurgeon withdrew from it in 1887.[42] Lloyd-Jones, a British Evangelical, never referred to himself as a Fundamentalist. But like Fundamentalists he criticized not only liberal theology but also alliances with liberals. In 1966 he issued a vain call to British Evangelicals to consider leaving their compromised denominations.[43]

Some Christians practice ecclesiastical separation from false teachings such as liberalism because they adhere to their theological or denominational distinctives in addition to the fundamentals of the Faith. In this group are staunchly conservative Calvinists, Lutherans, Baptists, and others. They also treat liberalism as a non-Christian religion and refuse to have anything to do with it. Usually, though, Christians in these groups differ with Fundamentalists. Sometimes that disagreement is over a matter such as personal separation. Many Reformed (Calvinistic) Christians reject prohibitions on tobacco or alcohol. They claim such questions are matters of Christian liberty to be decided by the individual Christian.[44]

More often these Christians think Fundamentalists do not require enough "fundamentals." They believe the boundaries of Christian fellowship should be narrower. The Protestant Reformed Churches of America, for example, is a small, Calvinistic, strictly separatist body. A writer in this denomination criticizes Fundamentalism for not carrying its essentials far enough. He says "that we would add to the list of fundamental truths many more truths, such as the truth of sovereign predestination, the truths of the five points of Calvinism, and the truth of the covenant."[45] In explaining why the Lutheran Church–Missouri Synod did not work with Fundamentalism, Milton Rudnick says that Fundamentalists stress points of agreement and "agree to disagree" about other points so that they may work or even worship together. "Missouri Synod Lutherans considered this controlling principle of Fundamentalism completely unacceptable and even sinful," Rudnick writes. Christians must observe all that Christ commands, he argues, such as the Lutheran views of the sacraments.[46] Baptist David E. Gonnella says that Fundamentalists err in not including baptism by immersion and other Baptist distinctives in their list of fundamentals. "I further submit," he says, "that fundamentalism is nothing more than a ploy of Satan . . . to dilute New Testament doctrine and practice."[47] For these Christians, Fundamentalists are either not Calvinistic enough, not Lutheran enough, or not Baptist enough. Yet these believers unquestionably practice separation from unbelief.

Conclusion

At least two themes mark the history of Fundamentalism: the idea of doctrinal "fundamentals" and the practice of separation. We discussed in Chapter 4 (pp. 42-43) the difference between a fundamental doctrine and a matter of interpretation. In the course of this chapter we have mentioned some of the doctrines defended by Fundamentalists: the inerrancy and authority of the Bible, Christ's deity and virgin birth, His vicarious atonement and resurrection, and the biblical teaching about Creation. Adherence to these and other fundamental doctrines has unquestionably characterized Fundamentalism.

Fundamentalism is also a movement characterized by its practice of separation. More than that, it has attempted to practice separation in a balanced manner. Groups such as Protestant Reformed Churches and the Lutheran Church–Missouri Synod, as we noted, also practice a form of separation. Yet unlike Fundamentalists, they add denominational and interpretational distinctives as tests of fellowship. Furthermore, some separatists with a strong denominational bias tend to overlook problems with a person or group of the same denomination if that person or group is "right" on denominational distinctives. Fundamentalism, ideally, insists that fundamental doctrines—not matters of interpretation—are the only beliefs that may be required of a Christian brother. Fundamentalism does not, however, allow the surrender of fundamental doctrines to accommodate anyone.

Fundamentalism is not perfect. Critics will always be able to cite shortcomings in the practices of Fundamentalists. The question, however, should be the central beliefs of the movement. Are there truths so essential to Christianity that they cannot be denied without destroying Christianity? Should these essentials be the basis of Christian fellowship? If the answer to these questions is yes, then Fundamentalists have a strong case to offer in defense of their practices. As the chapters that follow will demonstrate by contrast, Fundamentalism is virtually the only movement that maintains a testimony to the practice of biblical separation.

Liberalism
Chapter 7

Why do people believe what they believe? One basic reason is the authority they appeal to. In medieval Europe, the standard authority was the church and the Bible as interpreted by the church. Not only in religion but also in philosophy, politics, the arts, and all other fields of endeavor, the church was assumed to have the answer to every problem. People also assumed that it was God's answer the church was giving, but the church decided what that answer was.

In the Reformation in the 1500s, leaders such as Martin Luther and John Calvin demonstrated that what the church was saying was sometimes *not* what God was saying. The reformers did so by pointing out that the Bible, as God's Word, was an authority sufficient by itself to reveal God's message. "Scripture alone" was one of the themes of the reformers. At his famous appearance at the Diet of Worms, Luther told Emperor Charles V and his court, "Unless therefore I am convinced by the testimony of Scripture, or by the clearest reasoning—unless I am persuaded by means of the passages I have quoted, and unless they thus render my conscience bound by the Word of God, *I cannot and I will not retract,* for it is unsafe for a Christian to speak against his conscience. *Here I stand; I can do no other; may God help me. Amen.*"[1]

The Reformation's stress on the Bible, however, was not the end of the discussion of authority. Following the Reformation was the Age of Reason in the 1600s and 1700s. In this period reason displaced the Bible as an authority. In this post-Reformation age and its stress on reason, we find the roots of the many movements that go under the name *liberalism.*

Philosophical Background of Liberalism

An expression of the Age of Reason was the Enlightenment, a reexamination of the past and indeed of all knowledge in the light of human reason. "We should never allow ourselves to be persuaded of anything," philosopher René Descartes (1596-1650) said, "except by the evidence of our reason." Now in deciding questions of philosophy, politics, the arts—and religion—people looked to reason, not the church or the Bible. Leaders of the Enlightenment especially saw science as the great means of discovering sure knowledge. Some thinkers of this period claimed to be Christians looking for what God had to say, but they maintained that they would find God's Word not through revelation (the Bible) but through reason.

But how exactly does reason work? More particularly, where does knowledge come from? Does knowledge come through mental processes alone or is it somehow tied to our senses and experiences? Philosophers debated these questions. Descartes said that pure reason alone was enough. He believed, for example, that he could prove his own existence by the very fact that he thought. "I think, therefore I am" was his famous declaration. Scotsman David Hume (1711-76), on the other hand, said only experiences received through the senses could provide knowledge.

An answer to this dilemma was offered by the German philosopher Immanuel Kant (1724-1804). He agreed with Hume that sensory experience is necessary for scientific knowledge—knowledge about things in time and space. But Kant also said that reason played a role in knowledge. The human mind combines sensory experiences with *a priori* understandings (facts perceived as true before and apart from experience) to formulate valid scientific knowledge. The mind plays a role in shaping sensory experiences into knowledge. Furthermore, Kant said there is another realm beyond time and space, a realm of ideas, or "things in themselves." Here reason cannot operate; there is no "data" for reason to examine. Faith is the only way to understand "things in themselves," and you cannot demonstrate the truth of faith through scientific or mathematical proof. Instead, Kant said, the realm of things in themselves is validated by what he called "the categorical imperative." We would probably describe the categorical imperative as conscience, a universal sense of right and wrong.

Let us quickly say that we have greatly simplified Kant's ideas. His views sparked a revolution in philosophical thought in ways far beyond what we have discussed. What is important to our discussion is how Kant's ideas spurred the growth of religious liberalism. The things of God (His existence and attributes, e.g.) are not perceptible to the senses, Kant says. They lie in the realm of things in themselves, that realm of faith where reason does not operate. Faith, in other words, cannot be based on rational proof.

Kant's views had two important consequences for religious studies. First, he made whatever lies within the realm of the senses fair game for the applying of reason. We cannot know anything about God from reason, but we can apply rational methods to the study of the Bible as one of the phenomena available to our senses. In fact, we can thoroughly criticize the Scripture with the knowledge that we can never really damage faith, according to Kant's scheme. Second, the appeal to the categorical imperative based religious truth upon something *within* man and his experience. Religious truth could not be something revealed to man from above. Also, because it is inward, religion is ultimately about morality. Kant says religion "is to consist not in knowing or considering what God does or has done for our salvation but in what we must do to become worthy of it."[2] This position is the exact opposite of the Bible's teaching concerning grace, but it became a driving force behind the conclusions of many liberals.

Other ideas combined with Kant's philosophy to form modern religious liberalism. We mentioned in the last chapter how Charles Darwin's theory of biological evolution shook the intellectual world after *Origin of Species* came out in 1859. Also, German philosopher Georg Hegel popularized a scheme in which history is moving along a path of inevitable progress. (Karl Marx adapted Hegel's ideas as the basis for Communism.) The ideas of Darwin and Hegel led scholars to assume mankind's inevitable progress as virtually a law of science. These concepts of Kant, Darwin, and Hegel—religious truth being internal to man, evolution, and the inevitability of progress—contributed significantly to the rise of liberalism.

Rationalism and Higher Criticism

Beginning rather cautiously in the 1700s, rationalistic Bible scholars began to subject the Scripture to their scrutiny. The professed goal was to discover through historical research a solid foundation for religious belief and practice. Unfortunately, the result was not certainty but a confusing mixture of human opinions.

The term *criticism* is usually applied to scholarly study of the Bible.[3] *Lower criticism,* also called *textual criticism,* is the study of the surviving manuscripts of the Bible. Textual critics endeavor to determine the exact reading of the original Scripture by a careful study of all available manuscripts. *Higher criticism* is the study of the content of the Bible itself, dealing with questions of the authorship, date, and literary structure of the books of the Bible. Despite its name, biblical criticism is not necessarily critical. A Bible-believing scholar who studies the manuscripts of the Bible or carefully studies the content and structure of a book of the Bible is using biblical criticism in a responsible manner. A believing scholar, for example, might make an intensive study of the Epistle to the Hebrews to argue that the apostle Paul was or was not its author. The problem with biblical criticism comes when liberal higher critics with their wrong assumptions study the Bible in a way that undermines its authority. Such critics say that we should study the Bible just as we would any other book. Conservative scholar J. B. Lightfoot replied that we should study a book in light of what it claims to be—and the Bible declares itself to be the Word of God.

This critical study took different forms. Borrowing ideas from Hegel, Ferdinand Christian Baur offered a theory for the evolutionary development of Christianity. Baur said that originally Christianity was a kind of reformed Judaism, represented by Peter. This system met and clashed with Greek philosophy, represented by the teachings of Paul. The resulting synthesis was early Christianity. Later Christianity evolved further into Catholicism, Protestantism, and so on. Another popular historical study was the "search for historical Jesus." Critics assumed that the New Testament account of Christ was encrusted with legends. Therefore, they sought to rediscover the "true" Jesus of history. "Unreasonable" teachings such as Christ's miracles, virgin birth, and deity all gave way until critics had constructed a first-century philosopher and teacher who had little to do with the Christ presented in the Gospels.

The Old Testament received similar treatment. Critics particularly sought to uncover the various sources allegedly used in compiling the books of the Old Testament. The most famous example is the critical treatment of the Pentateuch. Building on the work of earlier scholars, Julius Wellhausen (1844-1918) theorized that the books credited to Moses were actually written over a period of centuries by combining different sources. The two oldest sources, although still not going back to the time of Moses, each used a different name for God: *Jehovah* and *Elohim.* These sources were called "J" and "E." A later source from the era of King Josiah added the legal requirements, such as those found in Deuteronomy; hence, it was called "D." Finally, after the Babylonian captivity, a team of priestly editors brought all these sources together into the five books we know today; this priestly work represented the "P" document. Wellhausen offered his JEDP theory in spite of the fact that Christ Himself said Moses was the author of the Pentateuch. Underlying all of this study—Old Testament and New—was an evolutionary view of history. Judaism and later Christianity had developed from simple, crude systems of belief into more complex forms. There was no idea of God giving a complete revelation to His people.

There was a strong emphasis on morality and good works in nineteenth-century liberalism. Albrecht Ritschl (1822-89) represented this tendency. Following Kant, he said we cannot really know or prove the "facts" (or doctrines) of Christianity. All we can know are the value judgments we can make about those facts. For example, we cannot know, says Ritschl, that Jesus Christ made an atonement for our sin to the Father. All we can know is that Jesus' death moves us to love as He loved and to serve our fellow man. Ritschl therefore also represented the liberal tendency to stress building the kingdom of God on earth.

The climax of nineteenth-century liberalism came with Adolf von Harnack (1851-1930). Harnack believed that Christianity had a kernel of truth covered by a husk of legend. He saw his task as removing the husk. By the time he had finished, Harnack had reduced Christ's teaching to three main principles: the need to proclaim and establish the kingdom of God, the fatherhood of God and the brotherhood of all men, and an ethic of loving God and loving your neighbor as yourself.[4]

Even this brief survey reveals a host of doctrinal deviations by liberalism from the Christian faith. The authority of the Bible was quickly discarded. Soon followed everything else that was "unreasonable"—the miracles of Scripture, for example. Liberals assaulted the biblical presentation of the person and work of Christ. Jesus was no longer God incarnate. Instead, He was simply a man who was "divine" in that He had a superior conception of God and God's will. His death was not a payment for sin but instead an example of sacrificial love. Liberals believed that God dwelt in all His creation in some fashion. Therefore in every man is a "spark of divinity." All that a person needs to do to become a child of God is to fan that spark into a flame. Such were the general characteristics of the system that came to America.[5]

Liberalism in America

Religious liberalism was far advanced in Europe before it came to America. Before the Civil War, the only important form of liberalism in the United States was Unitarianism. The Unitarians denied the deity of Christ, His atonement, and other essential doctrines. But Unitarians were in their own separate denomination. After the Civil War, liberalism began to invade the major Evangelical Protestant denominations.[6]

Liberalism appeared first in the schools of America. Baptist William Newton Clarke (1841-1912) is often said to have written the first liberal systematic theology in America, *An Outline of Christian Theology* (1898). Even more influential was William Rainey Harper (1856-1906). As president of the University of Chicago, he made that university and its divinity school a major center of liberalism in the United States. Even before the Fundamentalist-Modernist controversy, conservatives were criticizing the liberalism of the University of Chicago[7] and founding conservative seminaries to counteract its effects.

From the schools, liberalism went into the pulpits. Some early liberals began accommodating evolution in their sermons. Henry Ward Beecher (1813-87) was one of the first to try to cross evolution with Christianity. The great pulpit representative of liberalism, however, was Harry Emerson Fosdick (1878-1969). Fosdick was an eloquent and learned defender of the new liberal theology in sermons and articles. His *Guide to Understanding the Bible*[8] was a leading—and readable—introduction to liberal views, and his popular radio program carried liberalism into homes across America. Although a Baptist, Fosdick was serving the First Presbyterian Church in 1922, where he preached the sermon "Shall the Fundamentalists Win?" and touched off the Fundamentalist-Modernist controversy within the Presbyterian Church. Fosdick eventually became the founding pastor of Riverside Church in New York, one of the major liberal churches in the country.

Another expression of liberalism was the social gospel. The father of the social gospel was Walter Rauschenbusch (1861-1918). He taught that the gospel needed to be applied to social institutions. Accepting the teachings of liberal higher criticism, Rauschenbusch redefined the gospel. He denied the importance of Adam's fall (thus ignoring the root of all human sin) and made little of man's need of grace. He acknowledged the need for individual redemption from sin, but he did not refer to the biblical conception of salvation. Instead, he saw sin as an offense against man more than God and defined salvation as a process characterized by a life of love and service. Therefore, Rauschenbusch could speak of the "salvation" of social institutions. By this, he meant bringing all social organizations under the law of Christ. The goal of the social gospel was to build the kingdom of God on earth by human effort. Unsurprisingly, the phrase "social gospel" ultimately came to mean a system of social reform that had little or nothing to do with the redemption of souls through the atonement of Jesus Christ.[9]

The result of the growth of liberalism in the United States was the distortion of biblical Christianity. Neo-orthodox writer H. Richard Niebuhr pointedly satirized the liberal message: "A God without wrath brought men without sin into a kingdom without judgment through the ministrations of a Christ without a cross."[10]

Evolving Liberalism

Considering its evolutionary foundation, it is not surprising that liberalism continued to develop. The first major revision in American liberalism came in the 1930s after the Fundamentalist-Modernist controversy. Neo-Liberalism, as it was called, was a reaction to changing circumstances. Worsening world conditions—such as world war, the rise of dictatorships, the Great Depression—undercut the rosy optimism of the liberals. Further discoveries in archeology and biblical manuscripts likewise undercut some of the "assured results" of nineteenth-century higher criticism. Fosdick symbolized this transition to Neo-Liberalism in 1935 when he preached the sermon "The Church Must Go Beyond Modernism." Neo-Liberalism was to be more realistic, not naively optimistic, and would address the concerns of the common man in the pew. Unfortunately, it still did not address the common man's need of salvation.

One of the most important expressions of liberalism since World War II has been the ecumenical movement. *Ecumenical* means "universal" or "worldwide." The movement of that name is an attempt to unite all the churches around the world through organizations such as the World Council of Churches and (in the United States) the National Council of Churches. Unfortunately, the ecumenical movement seeks unity on a liberal basis. Ecumenists (those who support the movement) downplay doctrine and call for tolerance of many viewpoints. One organization promoting the movement, for example, took as its motto "Doctrine Divides, but

Service Unites." In recent years, liberal ecumenical organizations such as the World Council of Churches have even been opening their arms to non-Christian religions.

Liberalism continued to evolve into different forms, most of them more radical than the last. Terms such as "theology of hope," "process theology," and "secular theology" flew about in scholarly circles. The depths seemed to be reached in the 1960s with the short-lived "death of God" theology, an extreme form of secular theology. Theologians of this school actually said that the concept of God had no relevance for modern man and should be abandoned.[11]

Yet the 1960s saw the beginnings of even greater radicalism. In attempts to make theology "relevant," theologians began to mix political and social ideologies with their religious systems. Liberation theology was an example of a political theology. Borrowing heavily from Marxism, liberation theologians argued that God was on the side of the poor and oppressed. Therefore, Christians must devote themselves to relieving oppression, even to the point of supporting violent revolutions. Liberation theology had great appeal among Roman Catholic theologians in Latin America and black theologians in the United States. Feminist theology based its approach on the growing interest in a gender-dominated view of history. History is supposedly the story of the oppression of women, and theology is a tool for ending that oppression. Feminist theologians rejected traditional Christianity as the product of a biased, male-dominated, patriarchal society.

Ironically, in the latter half of the twentieth century, liberalism began to face a challenge that denied its ideological basis. Postmodernism, as it is known, had nothing to do with theological Modernism. Instead it was an attack on the basis of all modern thought. Postmodernism denied the rationalist basis of the Enlightenment. Human reason does not lead to a single unified view of reality, postmodernists argued, and scientific study is not a sure means to truth. Postmodernism takes Kant's ideas of how the individual perceives reality and makes "truth" a matter for the individual. "There are no facts, only interpretations" is a summary of postmodernist teaching. Postmodernism therefore denies the validity of liberalism's supporting structure, but it is no greater friend to orthodoxy. Liberalism looks to the collective knowledge of humanity as an authority whereas postmodernism looks to the interpretations of the individual as the authority. Many descendants of classic liberal theology, such as feminist theology and black theology, rely on postmodernist ideas.[12]

Evaluation of Liberalism

To say the least, liberalism is more diverse in its forms than Fundamentalism. But all forms of liberalism share a common problem: All place human authority over biblical authority. Even postmodernist systems that reject the Enlightenment's belief in science and reason still base authority on the individual's reason and perceptions.

The question is what is our starting point—divine authority or human reason? As Christians, we believe that the revelation of God is superior to human reason. Is the Bible the revelation of God? You cannot argue this point by reason (as some conservative theologians have tried to do) to show the reasonableness or authoritativeness of Scripture. Otherwise you are still setting up reason over God's revelation by saying that reason must prove that the Bible is God's revelation. Roman Catholics appeal to the authority of the church to establish the Bible's authority. "I would not even believe in the Gospels," said Jesuit missionary Francis Xavier, "were the Holy Church to forbid it."

Bible-believing Protestants look to the self-authenticating Scripture as their authority. The mind and the ways of God are beyond human comprehension (Rom. 11:33-34); on this point Immanuel Kant was right. The basis on which a person accepts God's Word as true is the internal witness of the Holy Spirit. Paul explained this matter in I Corinthians 2, concluding, "But the natural man receiveth not the things of the Spirit of God: for they are foolishness unto him: neither can he know them, because they are spiritually discerned" (I Cor. 2:14). For the Christian, reason must presuppose faith. In the words of Anselm of Canterbury (1033-1109), "For I do not seek to understand that I may believe, but I believe in order to understand. For this also I know,—that unless I believed, I should not understand."[13] Using God-given reason submitted to the authority of Scripture is the truly Christian way.

This denial of biblical authority is the root of liberal errors on the fundamentals. They saw their rational conclusions about religion as authoritative, or they looked to the Bible as it inspired religious experiences, which were then authoritative. Either way, the authority lay within man and not God's revealed Word. Liberalism therefore discarded teachings that did not accord with reason or were not validated by the liberal's own religious experience. As a result, they discarded the cardinal doctrines of the Faith.[14]

Jesus said of false teachers, "Ye shall know them by their fruits" (Matt. 7:16). The moral bankruptcy of liberalism is an example of such fruit. The early liberals were often very moral men and women. Modernists supported prohibition in America with as much fervor as the Fundamentalists did. But much of liberalism has grown more immoral with the passing of years. Acceptance of sexual relations outside of marriage, the ordination of homosexuals to the ministry—these and other fruits reveal the true nature of liberalism. Jude well summarized the moral character of such false teachers: "Clouds they are without water, carried about of winds; trees whose fruit withereth, without fruit, twice dead, plucked up by the roots; raging waves of the sea, foaming out their own shame; wandering stars, to whom is reserved the blackness of darkness for ever" (vv. 12-13). As Jude says, they "walk after their own ungodly lusts" (v. 18).

Liberalism is, in short, "another gospel." When Machen wrote his great defense of orthodoxy, he did not title it "Fundamentalism and Liberalism" but "*Christianity* and Liberalism." When he preached a response to Fosdick's "Shall the Fundamentalists Win?" Clarence Macartney did not title his message "Shall the Modernists Win?" but "Shall *Unbelief* Win?" Liberalism is not true Christianity, and we should treat it as we would any false teaching.

Some may consider such a blanket statement about liberals too sweeping. In particular, it appears presumptuous to judge the eternal destiny of professing Christians. We would not underestimate the seriousness of such false teaching. If, as the Bible says, doctrines such as the incarnation of Christ (II John 7-9) and His resurrection (I Cor. 15:12-19) are essential to the Christian faith, then individual liberals are, to say the least, in a precarious position. But, as Machen replied to the same charge, "we are not presuming to say whether such and such an individual man is a Christian or not. God only can decide such questions; no man can say with assurance whether the attitude of certain individual 'liberals' toward Christ is saving faith or not. But one thing is perfectly plain—whether or not liberals are Christians, it is at any rate perfectly clear that liberalism is not Christianity."[15]

Neo-orthodoxy
Chapter 8

As the Fundamentalists and the Modernists were battling for control of the major denominations in the 1920s, a system of theology other than Fundamentalism was beginning to criticize the liberal approach. Called *Neo-orthodoxy* (meaning "new orthodoxy"), this system claimed to be able to reconcile the Enlightenment's world view with orthodox Christianity. "The fundamentalist has something to say to his world," says one Neo-orthodox writer, "but he has lost the ability to say it. The modernist knows how to speak to his age, but he has nothing to say."[1] Although not truly orthodox, this movement had a tremendous effect on American religion and continues to affect even supposedly conservative Christianity.

Background of Neo-orthodoxy

Neo-orthodoxy describes itself as "orthodoxy rethought and reinterpreted for our times."[2] In general, Neo-orthodoxy accepted the revolution in thought brought about by the Enlightenment. The Neo-orthodox did not question scientific theories such as evolution and accepted the results of rationalistic higher criticism. They feared, however, that liberalism was abandoning the essential truths of Christianity, such as a notion of sin, God's transcendence, and the need of redemption. The Neo-orthodox revived the language of orthodoxy—but its critics charged that it changed the meaning of the language.[3]

The forerunner of Neo-orthodoxy was Danish philosopher and theologian Søren Kierkegaard (1813-55). Called the Father of Christian existentialism, Kierkegaard is like Kant in that his beliefs are complex and difficult to summarize. In brief, according to existentialism, every one of us faces the inescapable fact that we exist, and our existence is the basic truth of life. We find meaning in life not from some authority but from ourselves—from our own decisions and actions. Life itself has no purpose or meaning, so we create our own meaning by our actions. At its most extreme, existentialism holds that truth is completely subjective. There is no such thing as absolute truth; each individual develops his own truth.

It is the desire to find meaning in life apart from reason that gives rise to "Christian existentialism." Because Kierkegaard agreed with Kant that reason cannot lead men to God, he thought that a man must make a blind leap of faith and commit himself to God without—or even in spite of—reason. Then and only then can a person live an authentic Christian life. Often this leap of faith results from a major internal crisis. Neo-orthodoxy is therefore often referred to as the theology of crisis.

Karl Barth

We will focus particularly on Karl Barth (1896-1968) because of his importance as a leader in formulating the ideas of Neo-orthodoxy. Also, Barth is often considered the most conservative of the major Neo-orthodox leaders. If he cannot bear up under scriptural scrutiny, then it is unlikely that any other major leader of Neo-orthodoxy can.[4]

Born in Switzerland, Barth attended seminary in Germany, where he embraced liberalism. In serving as pastor of a church in Switzerland, however, he found liberalism inadequate to meet the needs of his people in the troubled era of World War I. In the midst of great inner struggle, Barth wrote a commentary on the book of Romans (1919) that became the first major document of Neo-orthodoxy. Later, as a university lecturer and prolific writer, Barth maintained his position as leader of the movement.

Barth rejected many ideas of liberalism. He denied natural theology, for example, saying that God cannot be known through nature by human reason. Instead, God is "wholly other"—completely transcendent and set apart from His creation. Only as God reveals Himself can anyone know Him. Rather than having a spark of divinity in their hearts, as liberals claimed, humans are sinful and separated from God. Only as God chooses to come to an individual can he be saved from his sin.

These concepts sound orthodox, hence the name "Neo-*orthodoxy.*" However, there was definitely a "new" side to Barth's teachings as well. The main charge laid against the Neo-orthodox is an inadequate view of Scripture. The Bible is *not* an inerrant revelation of God in their view. Instead, it is simply a witness to revelation, a means that God can use to communicate His revelation to men. Only as God meets with the individual in the Bible does it become God's Word to him. Illustrating Barth's view of Scripture is an interview from 1934 between Barth and American Evangelical Donald Grey Barnhouse. Barnhouse recounts the following discussion of the Bible:

> "You say that the Bible is the only source of revelation, but do you believe that all of the Bible is God's revelation?"
>
> Dr. Barth had a book in his hand. He divided a page with a gesture of his hand and said, "If this part of the Bible speaks to me, it is God's Word to me." And then indicating the other part of the page, "If this part does not speak to me, it is not God's Word to me."
>
> That is enough to make some people's hair stand on end, but I was convinced that there was something more than appeared upon the surface of his speech, so I said, "But Doctor, suppose the part that hasn't spoken to you really speaks to me. Is it then God's Word?"
>
> "Certainly," he replied. "It is then God's Word for you."
>
> "And do you believe that the part which is God's Word to me may someday become God's Word to you?"
>
> "Of course. Anything in the Bible may become God's Word to me."[5]

Because he saw the Bible as an errant, human book that only testified to God's Word, Barth accepted the idea of historical criticism of the Bible. In fact, he claimed it was an indication of God's power that He could use such an error-filled, limited book of human origin to convey His revelation to man.

Critics have also accused Barth of teaching two kinds of "history." For Barth, critics say, events such as the Resurrection take place in the realm of "super history" but do not take place in the world of everyday events as we know them. In other words, according to this charge, Barth can say Christ truly rose from the grave, but he does not mean it in the same historical sense as when he says that Napoleon invaded Russia in 1812.

Evangelical Bernard Ramm staunchly defends Barth against this charge and cites examples from Barth's writings.[6] Cornelius Van Til, on the other hand, argues just as strongly that Barth does make such a distinction, quoting extensively from Barth.[7] The fact that you can read Barth's own writings and still not be able to determine whether this charge is valid indicates how difficult and complex his ideas are. Reading Barth is rather like looking at a piece of abstract art: each viewer sees something different in the picture. However, even if Barth does not see two "kinds" of history, no one denies that he is still willing to view parts of Scripture as "myth" or "saga." He does not believe that Genesis 1-3 is historical, for example. Consequently, the fall of man is not the result of a real individual named Adam eating from a real tree in a real place called Eden. Man is simply naturally sinful because he is separated from God and has always been separated from God.

Barth discussed the idea of salvation, but he stressed Christ's incarnation instead of His atonement as the basis. Some of his statements concerning the extent of salvation led to the charge of universalism—that he believed everyone will be saved. The fact that Barth was never able to answer the charge indicates that there is some basis for it. He said during a series of lectures, "I should like . . . to answer a question which has been put to me several times during these weeks: 'Are you not aware that many are sitting in this class who are not Christians?' I have always laughed and said: 'That makes no difference to me.' It would be quite dreadful if the faith of Christians should aim at sundering and separating one man from the others. It is in fact the strongest motive for collecting men and binding them together."[8]

We have dealt with Barth in detail because, as we said, he is not only typical of Neo-orthodoxy but also is reputed to be the most orthodox. There are more problems with his theology than are listed here. His view of the Trinity, for example, sounds a great deal like the ancient modalistic heresy—that the persons of the Godhead are simply three manifestations of the same being. We have focused, however, on those views on which there is little debate even from Barth's defenders. His view of Scripture, his denial of the historicity of Adam and the fall of man, and his tendencies toward universalism all indicate that his "Neo-orthodoxy" is not particularly orthodox.

Other Neo-orthodox Leaders

Karl Barth was the major leader of Neo-orthodoxy, but there were other notable figures as well. Swiss theologian Emil Brunner (1889-1966) emerged in the public eye about the same time as Barth. In fact, he was initially better known in America than Barth and was the one who really introduced Neo-orthodoxy to the United States.[9] Brunner disagreed with Barth concerning the place of natural theology. Barth said that God revealed Himself only through the Bible; Brunner claimed that God could reveal Himself through other means, such as nature or history. Brunner also helped popularize a major Neo-orthodox concept, that revelation is "personal," not "propositional." In other words, God reveals Himself personally to an individual. He never reveals Himself through propositions, that is, statements of fact about Himself. Hordern illustrates Brunner's view this way. To say that Jesus is the Christ, the Messiah, is not revelation. It is only a proposition that points to revelation because it points to Christ.[10] Concepts such as God's holiness and almighty power do not reveal God but only point to Him.

The leading representatives of Neo-orthodoxy in the United States were two brothers: Reinhold (1892-1970) and H. Richard Niebuhr (1894-1962).[11] Their version of Neo-orthodoxy is sometimes called realistic theology because it seems to take a more realistic view of man's nature than traditional liberalism. Reinhold was probably the more influential of the brothers. Ryrie suggests that he represents the Neo-orthodox preservation of the social gospel (discussed in Chapter 7) because he was so concerned with social ethics.[12] Both Martin Luther King Jr. and President Jimmy Carter claimed to have been deeply influenced by Niebuhr's writings. Although willing to acknowledge the truth of man's sinfulness, he denies the biblical basis for human sin. He criticizes the "absurd notion" that "man's sinfulness is determined by the Biblical account of the fall of Adam." Niebuhr argues instead that the reality of sinfulness "is supported by overwhelming evidence taken both from a sober observation of human behavior and from introspective analysis."[13] In a manner typical of Neo-orthodoxy, Niebuhr redefines biblical terms, such as saying that original sin "is not so much an inherited corruption as an inevitable taint upon the spirituality of a finite creature."[14]

Other famous theologians are sometimes associated with Neo-orthodoxy. Paul Tillich (1886-1965) and New Testament critic Rudolf Bultmann (1884-1976) are occasionally labeled Neo-orthodox, but they really belong to the most radical wing of liberalism. Another name that often comes up in connection with Neo-orthodoxy is Dietrich Bonhoeffer (1906-45). A German theologian and student of Barth, Bonhoeffer became caught up in resistance to the Nazis. He was eventually executed for his part in a plot to assassinate Hitler. Since he died before his ideas were fully developed, it is difficult to know where to classify him theologically. In the 1960s, however, the "death of God" theologians (discussed in Chapter 7) claimed his writings as their inspiration.[15]

Evaluation of Neo-orthodoxy

As this survey of Neo-orthodox views demonstrates, the movement has serious shortcomings. As is the case with liberalism, the root of Neo-orthodoxy's problems is the movement's inadequate view of the authority of Scripture. The truly orthodox Christian can never accept the relativistic view of revelation reflected by statements such as Hordern's: "God's Word never consists of black marks on the pages of a book called the Bible; God's Word is the living Word which he speaks through the Bible and to which man must respond by saying yes or no."[16] The authority for religion, according to Neo-orthodoxy, lies within the individual as God speaks to Him.

From that starting point Neo-orthodoxy goes on to more serious errors. There is a definite tendency to find "truth" in the Bible without allowing the book itself to be true. The Neo-orthodox theologian or minister may allow that the story of Noah reflects the truth that God hates sin, but do not expect him to believe that the tale of the ark, the animals, and the worldwide Flood is actually true. These word games are what lead Charles Ryrie to conclude, "Neoorthodoxy is a theological hoax. It attempts to preserve the message of the Bible while denying the facts of the Bible."[17]

What confuses matters for the conservative Christian is that Neo-orthodoxy often sounds good. Consider H. Richard Niebuhr's blunt and accurate summary of liberalism, quoted on page 98. Many Evangelicals likewise quote Bonhoeffer's indictment of "cheap grace": "Cheap grace is the preaching of forgiveness without requiring repentance, baptism without church discipline, communion without confession, absolution without personal confession. Cheap grace is grace without discipleship, grace without the cross, grace without Jesus Christ, living and incarnate."[18] Could this perhaps be a pointed way of stating the principle that Paul enunciated in Romans 6:15: "What then? shall we sin, because we are not under the law, but under grace?"

But as Cornelius Van Til notes, "Final alliances and final hostilities depend upon the content rather than the sound of words."[19] Revelation is not simply personal but is also propositional. Propositions do not save, but they indeed describe the person who does save. Alan Cairns writes that "orthodox theology has always recognized the necessity of a personal encounter with God in and through the Lord Jesus Christ. Mere knowledge about God cannot save the soul. A saving revelation of God must be such a personal revelation of Him and by Him to the heart as will impart new life and yield faith in Christ. But this personal revelation must have an objective and verifiable basis."[20]

As this last comment indicates, one of the great problems of Neo-orthodoxy is its subjectivism. In other words, Neo-orthodoxy does not give the believer something objective, something outside of himself, on which to base his faith; his internal thoughts, feelings, and convictions provide the basis for his faith. But this is unscriptural. Peter describes how he and the other apostles had actually seen and heard Jesus Christ (II Pet. 1:16-18). But he says, "We have also a more sure word of prophecy" (v. 19). The Scriptures, which "came not in old time by the will of man" but were the product as "holy men of God spake as they were moved by the Holy Ghost" (v. 21), are more certain than any experience, even an eyewitness account.

Likewise Luke, at the opening of his Gospel, describes how many had attempted to write an account "of those things which are most surely believed among us" (Luke 1:1). Far from arguing that a written account cannot communicate the revelation of God, Luke says to Theophilus that he desires "to write unto thee in order" (literally, "to write out in order for you") so "that thou mightest know the certainty of those things, wherein thou hast been instructed" (vv. 3-4). The idea of faith being a leap into the dark, as Kierkegaard maintained, is completely unbiblical. "In sharp contrast to all this, in Bible Christianity faith is not a leap in the dark. It is a step into the light."[21]

You may wonder, perhaps, what exactly Neo-orthodoxy has to do with you. A Bible professor once noted that he had never met anyone who was Neo-orthodox outside of a book. In fact, you are probably more likely to meet an outright liberal. But there are good reasons for noting the dangers of this movement. First of all, Neo-orthodoxy is an example of subtle error. (Indeed, the reason you may think that you have never met anyone who is Neo-orthodox may be that it is so hard to tell.) Jesus warned against wolves in sheep's clothing (Matt. 7:15). The fact that someone uses the correct terminology and criticizes false teachers does not necessarily mean that he is himself genuine.

Another danger is that some supposedly conservative and Evangelical Christians are embracing Neo-orthodoxy. Walter Martin criticizes Fundamentalists for lumping the Neo-orthodox together with Neo-Liberals as unbelievers.[22] We have mentioned already how noted Evangelical writer Bernard Ramm staunchly defends Karl Barth in his book *After Fundamentalism*. Ramm says that Christians should adopt Barth's methodology but not necessarily his conclusions.

Most often, some Evangelicals are charged with following some form of the Neo-orthodox teaching on Scripture. John Woodbridge says Jack Rogers and Donald McKim in their study of inerrancy followed a Neo-orthodox view of the history of doctrine. He does not accuse Rogers and McKim themselves of being Neo-orthodox but of using the Neo-orthodox approach in their critique of inerrancy as a newly invented doctrine.[23] Some Evangelicals go further. Theologian Donald Bloesch, although critical of some aspects of the movement, writes that "it can be shown that I stand partly in both neo-evangelicalism and neo-orthodoxy, even though I belong mostly to catholic evangelicalism."[24] Neo-orthodoxy is still affecting the teachers and preachers that Christians hear and read, and thereby it affects church life in often subtle ways.[25]

It is probably not fair to assume that everyone who says "The Bible *contains* the Word of God" is Neo-orthodox. Some who hold to this position believe that there is objective revelation from God in the Bible mixed with historical and scientific error. To discern precisely what in the Bible really is the Word of God, however, such Christians must rely on human reason (the traditional liberal method) or intuition (the Neo-orthodox approach). In either case, humans are determining what is revelation and not letting revelation be the authority in their lives.

Even to call Neo-orthodoxy a deeply flawed system would probably be too generous, and Evangelicals—not to mention Fundamentalists—should be wary of it. Neo-orthodoxy is more accurately called, as Cornelius Van Til put it, "the new Modernism." Perhaps some orthodox believers have been attracted to Neo-orthodoxy because of its reputation for scholarly orthodoxy. But the Neo-orthodox system, as we concluded about liberalism in the previous chapter, is not biblical Christianity.

The New Evangelicalism
Chapter 9

In past chapters we have referred to *Evangelicalism* or the *New Evangelicalism* with only passing reference to what those terms mean. Although the word *evangelical* has a long history, it has come in the twentieth century to have a distinct meaning. Fundamentalists are technically Evangelicals, but the more precise use of that term identifies a position that consciously rejects part of the Fundamentalist position.

What's in a Name?

The word *evangelical* derives from *euangelion,* the Greek word for "good news" or "gospel." It is from this root that we derive other words such as *evangelize.* During the Reformation the Protestant churches were often called "evangelical." Even today in Germany the "Evangelical Church" refers to the state Lutheran Church.[1]

In Great Britain and America, the term *Evangelical* took on a new meaning in the 1700s as a result of Britain's Evangelical Awakening (led by John Wesley and George Whitefield) and America's Great Awakening. In English-speaking countries and some other parts of the world, *Evangelical* now refers to a Protestant with specific beliefs. Although there is no set definition of what an Evangelical believes, the following are among the most common tenets: the authority of Scripture alone in religious matters, the importance of the substitutionary atonement of Christ, a stress on the experience of the new birth and individual conversion, an emphasis on good works and holy living after conversion, and the evangelization of non-Christians.[2]

Fundamentalists obviously fall into this category. But since the 1950s the term *Evangelical* has come to denote something even more specific. As John Sanderson notes, "If anything, 'Evangelical' is a more Biblical word than 'Fundamentalist' since the former is derived from the word we translate 'Gospel.' But words take on new meanings and different emotional colorings."[3] Today the term *Evangelical* is a catch-all for "any non-Fundamentalist conservative who does not accept or practice the principle of ecclesiastical separation."[4] The reason for this narrow use of the term is the influence of a movement beginning in the 1940s called "the New Evangelicalism." That movement, and its influence, is the subject of this chapter.

Before we discuss this movement, however, we should mention a point concerning the term *New Evangelical.* Fundamentalists are virtually the only group that uses the term today. Most people who belong to what Fundamentalists call "New Evangelicalism" would see themselves as simply "Evangelical" without anything "New" about it. Fundamentalists, however, are loath to surrender the term *Evangelical* completely, and they want to note the disagreement over separation marked by the terms *Fundamentalist* and *New Evangelical.* Fundamentalists need to realize, however, that most of the people they call "New Evangelical" do not recognize the term. David Beale has suggested the aptly descriptive term *Broad Evangelicalism,* as distinguished from Fundamentalist Evangelicalism, but the term has not yet caught on.[5] Bowing to common usage, we will use the terms *Evangelical* and *New Evangelical* for the most part interchangeably in this chapter.

Rise of the New Evangelicalism

After the Fundamentalist-Modernist controversy, as we mentioned in Chapter 6, Fundamentalists began to develop their own network of independent schools, periodicals, mission boards, and denominations. But with this independence came a loss in national status. No longer were Fundamentalists part of the major denominations that dominated American religious life. *Fundamentalism* itself had become a negative term to most Americans, synonymous with bigotry and ignorance. A segment within Fundamentalism began to want to reform the movement and to change its image. Some Fundamentalists began to use the less controversial label *Evangelical.*

Historian Joel Carpenter points out how Fundamentalism faced two possible courses of "reform" in the 1940s. One way would be to "strengthen" Fundamentalism. Leaving the basic position of Fundamentalism unchanged, this approach would raise the intellectual level of Fundamentalist apologetics and theological writings. Also it would attempt to moderate the more caustic language that Fundamentalists had used in the heat of controversy. The other course of reform sought to "revise" Fundamentalism. This approach sought to take Fundamentalism in a different direction in scholarship and especially in regard to the matter of separation.[6] This second method became the philosophy of the New Evangelicalism. The spokesman for the movement was Harold J. Ockenga, sometimes called the Father of the New Evangelicalism. He was pastor of the historic Park Street Congregational Church in Boston and the first president of Fuller Theological Seminary. Supporting Ockenga in this effort were several other young Evangelical intellectuals, including Carl Henry, the founding editor of *Christianity Today.*[7]

The statements of Ockenga provide a summary of the basic views of the New Evangelicalism. Ockenga was one of the first to use the term *New Evangelicalism,* and he outlined the movement's basic beliefs in his foreword to Harold Lindsell's *Battle for the Bible.*[8] Those beliefs, and the Fundamentalist reaction to them, sparked a major controversy and division within the Fundamentalist ranks.

First, Ockenga spoke of New Evangelicalism's "determination to engage itself in the theological dialogue of the day" and the need for "the reengagement in the theological debate." The New Evangelicals believed that Fundamentalism was not conducting biblical study at a sufficiently high level of scholarship. There was a need, they said, for interchange with liberal scholars. As part of that move, several talented young Evangelicals began to attend prestigious graduate schools in America and Europe.

Fundamentalism is not opposed to intellectual study, and Christians need to be aware of all shades of scholarship. The question is what compromises are made to the Christian faith in order to achieve this "higher level" of scholarship. What is being surrendered by Christians in their efforts at "dialogue" with liberals? At first New Evangelicals protested that they simply wanted to compete with liberals in their own fields of study and to witness to them of Christ.[9] Fundamentalists, however, feared that the movement was heading toward acceptance of liberals as orthodox believers. Bob Jones Jr. wrote, "In effect, they [the New Evangelical leaders] said to the enemies of Christian faith, 'We will call you "Christian brothers" if you will call us "doctor," "professor," and "scholar." ' "[10] Sanderson mentions how critics feared that New Evangelicals would either absorb liberal beliefs or at least accommodate liberal ideas. He also notes that critics thought that the New Evangelicalism risked setting a bad precedent that would cause later generations to accept liberalism.[11] The passing of years has revealed the validity of these fears, as we shall see.

Second, Ockenga wrote of the need for "the reexamination of theological problems such as the antiquity of man, the universality of the Flood, God's method of creation, and others." Almost from the beginning, the New Evangelicals suggested accommodation toward evolutionary theory. The national embarrassment of the Scopes "Monkey Trial" was apparently still with them. Some questioned belief in Creationism, a young earth, and the Bible's account of Noah and the Flood. They did so heedless of the impact of such questions on the historicity of the Bible and on biblical teachings such as original sin and Christ's work as the Second Adam (Rom. 5:12-21; I Cor. 15:21-22, 45).

Third, Ockenga also issued a "summons to social involvement" and a "new emphasis upon the application of the gospel to the sociological, political, and economic areas of life." This belief was not originally a call to the liberal idea of the social gospel, although Fundamentalists were concerned when Ockenga said things such as, "There need be no disagreement between the personal gospel and the social gospel."[12] The social gospel (discussed in Chapter 7) downplayed or eliminated personal salvation in favor of social reform. The original New Evangelicals did not favor this kind of social gospel. They wanted to state what the Bible said concerning social issues, to denounce sin in any form it might take.

The years have seen a shift in social theory among some Evangelicals, however. Originally, it is clear that men such as Ockenga and Carl Henry sought a testimony on social issues that was based on the redemption of the individual through Christ. Henry, for example, wrote in 1947, "Only an anthropology and a soteriology that insists upon man's sinful lostness and the ability of God to restore the responsive sinner is the adequate key to the door of Fundamentalist world betterment."[13] As the years passed, younger Evangelicals began to stake out other positions that threatened to redefine the gospel. After surveying contemporary Christian attitudes toward social action, Robert Horton concludes that many Evangelicals view social action as a form of evangelism rather than a means to evangelism. Others, he points out, make social reform a part of the gospel itself.[14]

Such a position distorts the gospel by adding to it. Fundamentally, the gospel is the redemption of sinners by Jesus Christ through His atonement. "This is a faithful saying, and worthy of all acceptation, that Christ Jesus came into the world to save sinners" (I Tim. 1:15). There is a social dimension to Christianity (Matt. 5:13-16; Gal. 6:10), but it is a result of the salvation of individuals through the gospel, not part of the gospel itself. Furthermore, there is a danger that stress on social action can make the church a mere tool of conservative or liberal political factions.

Finally, and most important, Ockenga proclaimed a "ringing call for a repudiation of separation" and aimed for "the recapture of denominational leadership." Rather than pulling out of compromised associations, the New Evangelicals wanted to stay in the denominations and even reenter those that Fundamentalists had left. We have already reviewed many of the New Evangelical arguments against separation in Chapters 1-5. From the beginning, Fundamentalists protested that the New Evangelicalism was leading Christianity toward too close an identification with the world system. Unquestionably, the New Evangelicals were taking an attitude that although false teaching might be wrong, Christians could profitably work with false teachers themselves. The actions of these New Evangelical "reformers" led many Fundamentalists to reluctantly break fellowship with these Christians who rejected the scriptural teaching concerning separation from false teaching.

In a 1957 press release Ockenga not only set forth the ideology of the New Evangelicalism but also listed its main institutions. These included the National Association of Evangelicals, Fuller Theological Seminary, *Christianity Today* magazine, and the campaigns of Evangelist Billy Graham.[15] It was Graham who became the focus of the movement and its most influential leader.

Billy Graham and the New Evangelicalism

Understanding Billy Graham's contribution is essential to understanding the widespread impact of the New Evangelicalism. Many non-Fundamentalist Evangelicals do not fit the pattern found in the list of characteristics from Ockenga's writings. Some are Creationists who have little interest in interaction with liberal scholars and are suspicious of the involvement of the church in politics. In other words, on some points they too question the New Evangelicalism. This is why the label "New Evangelical" does not always fit. But these Evangelicals still are not considered Fundamentalists because of their acceptance of the methods and ministry of Billy Graham.[16]

Born in 1918, Graham was converted as a teenager and attended Bob Jones College, Florida Bible Institute, and Wheaton College. After graduating from Wheaton and following a brief period in the pastorate, he went into evangelism. Working as a staff evangelist for Youth for Christ after World War II, Graham began to build a reputation as a Fundamentalist preacher. In 1949 he held an evangelistic crusade in Los Angeles that had such remarkable effect that it made the newspapers and national magazines such as *Time*. He followed it up with notable campaigns first in Boston, then in other large cities across the country, and finally London in 1954. Conservative Christians rallied to Graham. It appeared to many that he might be leading the national, even worldwide, revival that many had been praying for.

Graham, however, became convinced that the New Evangelical approach being suggested by Ockenga would provide wider opportunities for proclaiming the gospel. He lent warm support in 1956 to the founding of *Christianity Today* as a voice for the New Evangelicalism. He agreed in 1958 to join the board of Fuller Theological Seminary, the leading educational institution of the New Evangelicalism. But the real turning point came with his New York campaign in 1957. Declaring that he would "go anywhere, sponsored by anybody, to preach the Gospel of Christ, if there are no strings attached to my message," Graham opened his campaign to liberals. He invited liberal ministers to participate, and he sent converts from his crusade into liberal churches.

Graham's support gave the New Evangelicalism a greater impact than it ever could have had through the more purely intellectual pursuits of Ockenga, Henry, and others. American Christians cherished evangelism and revival. They were far more willing to follow a renowned and successful evangelist than an assembly of seminary professors. It is probably no exaggeration to say that the New Evangelicalism never would have had the impact that it did without the influence of Billy Graham. Quite rightly Ockenga said that Graham "on the mass level is the spokesman of the convictions and ideals of the New Evangelicalism."[17]

The activities of Graham brought Evangelicals into cooperation with liberals but split conservative Christianity. We have already discussed in Chapter 6 how separatist Fundamentalists refused to go along with the new movement. They had protested the ideas of the New Evangelical intellectuals. But the actions of Graham sparked a final split.

Basically, Fundamentalists said efforts such as the Graham crusades treated liberals as Christian brethren. Interestingly, Millard Erickson, a defender of the New Evangelicalism, well sums up the Fundamentalist position. He says that Fundamentalists argue "that Graham, by cooperating with liberal churches and ministers, and having even such men as Norman Vincent Peale sit on the platform with him, is tacitly approving of the liberalism which they represent.

He is failing to distinguish, for the public, the spiritual value of nurture in a conservative church from that of a liberal church. He is sending converts back into liberal churches, where their spiritual zeal will be confused and they will be given stones instead of bread."[18]

Erickson and others, such as Robert O. Ferm,[19] defend Graham. Erickson asks whether Fundamentalists do not think that liberals need to hear the gospel too? And will not converts sent back into liberal churches "become leavening influences" in those churches?[20] Fundamentalists reply that they are delighted to see liberals confronted with the gospel but that presenting them as sponsors of an evangelistic campaign is not witnessing to liberals; it is instead persuading believers that false teachers are true brethren. Likewise sending converts back into false churches is not creating a leavening influence; it is like sending sheep into a wolfpack and asking them to try to reform the pack by their example.

The Separation Question and Decline

The gap between Fundamentalist and non-Fundamentalist Evangelicalism has only increased since the split in the 1950s. Initially, the differences revolved around the question of separation from false teachers. Since that time other issues have widened the breach. There are still some Evangelicals whose main disagreement with Fundamentalism is the matter of ecclesiastical separation. But there are others who have departed farther from biblical teaching and practice.

The first great battleground among Evangelicals was over the inerrancy of the Bible. The early New Evangelicals spoke of "a re-opening of the subject of biblical inspiration," but they meant a fuller defense of biblical infallibility against the teachings of Neo-orthodoxy.[21] It soon became apparent that some Evangelicals were denying the inerrancy of Scripture. In 1976 New Evangelical leader Harold Lindsell shook the Evangelical world with his book *The Battle for the Bible*. He detailed examples of how Evangelicals were abandoning inerrancy. One of the most controversial chapters was that on Fuller Theological Seminary, the flagship school of the New Evangelicalism where Lindsell had formerly taught.[22] Lindsell showed how some professors had annually signed a creed saying they believed in inerrancy, when in reality they did not. Fuller eventually dropped inerrancy from its creed altogether.

Also in the 1970s, the Evangelical world was unsettled by two books by Richard Quebedeaux: *The Young Evangelicals* (1974) and *The Worldly Evangelicals* (1978).[23] In these works, Quebedeaux reports a liberalization of the theological and social views of Evangelicals among the younger generation. Theologically, he notes an increased rejection of inerrancy, an openness to discussions with liberals and Marxists as a means of furthering the gospel, an acceptance of theistic evolution over biblical Creationism, and an embrace of some points of Neo-orthodoxy.[24] On moral issues, he cited defense of masturbation, a greater tolerance for divorce and remarriage, acceptance of abortion, more prevalent use of profanity among Christians, and acceptance of practicing homosexuals as believers.[25] These are but a sample of the views he says are becoming more prevalent among Evangelicals. Significantly, Quebedeaux titles the last chapter of his second book "Today's Evangelicals, Tomorrow's Liberals?"

Still, defenders of Evangelicalism could argue that Quebedeaux's evidence was anecdotal. In other words, he was simply compiling "horror stories" that represented only a fringe of the movement, not its mainstream. This excuse was less valid, however, in weighing James Davison Hunter's *Evangelicalism: The Coming Generation* (1987). Surveying students in nine Evangelical colleges and seven Evangelical seminaries, Hunter documents a shift in views.[26] Hunter's conclusions are not as shocking as Quebedeaux's. Attitudes of Evangelical students are still more conservative than those of secular students. But Hunter clearly documented a drift in the Evangelical movement. About half the students surveyed believe the Bible can err on matters of science or history.[27] About a third believe that those who have never heard of Christ or the gospel can still go to heaven.[28] On issues of personal morality, Hunter is able to demonstrate how great the change was from the past. In a 1951 survey, 46 percent of the students questioned thought that attending Hollywood movies was always morally wrong; in 1982 only 7 percent thought attending R-rated movies was always morally wrong. In 1951, 98 percent of the students thought drinking alcohol was wrong whereas in 1982 only 17 percent did.[29] Hunter also demonstrates that the teachers in such schools are generally more liberal in their views than the students.[30] So concerned were Evangelical leaders about the ramifications of Hunter's work that they held a conference to discuss it.[31]

A case study in the drift of Evangelicalism is the career of theologian Clark Pinnock. Originally, in the 1960s and early 1970s, Pinnock was a staunch defender of biblical inerrancy and wrote persuasively on the subject.[32] Then in the mid-1970s he began to shift. First, he abandoned his position on inerrancy and said that there were historical and scientific errors in the Scripture.[33] Then Pinnock abandoned the doctrine of hell, teaching instead that sinners are merely annihilated after death.[34] In 1997 Millard Erickson included Pinnock in his discussion of "postconservative evangelicalism." In addition to Pinnock's views of the Scripture and hell, Erickson noted his shift on the doctrine of God. Pinnock was now holding that God is not omniscient, knowing all things past, present, and future. For God to be omniscient would limit human freedom. Instead, God knows the past and present but can know only future possibilities.[35]

Not all Evangelicals are changing as much as Pinnock, of course. Furthermore, some New Evangelical leaders such as Lindsell and Ockenga have opposed this drift. But there is little question that the position of Evangelicalism has moved leftward. An increasingly widespread and particularly surprising example is an openness toward the idea of salvation apart from Christ. Even Billy Graham, long considered one of the more theologically conservative Evangelicals, has supported such a position. In a 1997 television interview, Graham said that God is "calling people out of the world for His name, whether they come from the Muslim world, or the Buddhist world, or the Christian world or the nonbelieving world, they are members of the Body of Christ because they've been called by God. They may not even know the name of Jesus but they know in their hearts that they need something that they don't have, and they turn to the only light that they have, and I think that they are saved, and that they're going to be with us in heaven."[36]

Evangelicals have sometimes accused Fundamentalists, unfortunately with good reason, with constantly splintering and splitting over nonessentials. But the New Evangelicals have more than justified Fundamentalist concerns that their openness to liberalism and their desire for respectability would lead Evangelical Christianity into theological error. The split between Fundamentalism and the New Evangelicalism began as a dispute over ecclesiastical separation.[37] It is becoming a divide over a number of crucial doctrines, at least in some circles of Evangelicalism. Fundamentalists find themselves forced to separate from other Evangelicals not simply over disobedience but over false doctrine.

"Neo-Fundamentalism"

One other theological movement belongs in this discussion of the New Evangelicalism. It has been called different names by different writers. Earle Cairns refers to it as "Open Fundamentalism" in contrast to the "Closed Fundamentalism" of militant separatists.[38] Fundamentalists themselves label it "Pseudo-Fundamentalism."[39] However, "Neo-Fundamentalism" is probably the closest to an accepted academic term.[40]

Neo-Fundamentalism took as its goal reforming Fundamentalism, much as the New Evangelicalism had sought to do. There are many parallels between the movements. Like the original New Evangelicals, the Neo-Fundamentalists moved in Fundamentalist circles and proclaimed their allegiance to the heritage of Fundamentalism. They argued that the movement had become too narrow and was not sufficiently active in social issues. The differences between it and the New Evangelicalism were, first of all, that Neo-Fundamentalism showed no interest in any ties to liberalism, as Billy Graham had. Furthermore, by social action, Neo-Fundamentalists meant greater involvement by Fundamentalists in behalf of conservative political causes.[41]

The most important formative figures in the movement were Jerry Falwell and, to a lesser extent, Jack Van Impe, both of whom typify the movement. Van Impe was an evangelist and television preacher well known in Fundamentalism. He had held numerous successful citywide campaigns and had addressed the first World Congress of Fundamentalists in 1976. In the late 1970s, however, he began to denounce what he called a hate movement among Fundamentalists. He claimed that Fundamentalists were majoring on (and separating over) minor issues. In 1984 he published the book *Heart Disease in Christ's Body* in which he outlined these charges and finalized his own break with separatist Fundamentalism.

Far more important to the Neo-Fundamentalist movement was Baptist pastor Jerry Falwell of Lynchburg, Virginia. A member of the Baptist Bible Fellowship (one of the largest independent Baptist groups), Falwell had begun to attract attention in the 1960s. The remarkable growth of his congregation, the Thomas Road Baptist Church, gave it one of the ten largest Sunday schools in America by 1969. He also benefited greatly in Fundamentalist circles from the warm support and promotion of John R. Rice in *The Sword of the Lord.*

Falwell achieved national renown after he founded the political action organization known as the Moral Majority in 1979. This organization was one of many conservative religious groups credited with helping elect Republican Ronald Reagan to the presidency in 1980. Falwell found himself famous but also under attack. Political liberals accused him of trying to force his religious beliefs on the United States. Fundamentalists charged him with compromising the Faith. Despite opposition, Falwell maintained an extensive national outreach through his television program, *The Old Time Gospel Hour;* his school, Liberty University; and his periodical, *The Fundamentalist Journal.*

Theologically, Neo-Fundamentalism was initially critical of New Evangelical tolerance and Billy Graham's cooperation with liberals.[42] The movement, however, bases its practice of separation on the distinction between first-degree and second-degree separation (discussed in Chapters 1 and 5). As a result, Neo-Fundamentalism rejects false teaching but is much less likely to separate from other Christians.[43] Neo-Fundamentalism insists strenuously on the cardinal doctrines of the Faith, especially the inerrancy of Scripture. But the movement uses this doctrinal stance as a basis for suggesting closer alliances between themselves and conservative Evangelicals dismayed by the excesses of the "worldly Evangelicals" described by Quebedeaux.[44] Part of their argument for this position parallels that of the New Evangelicals: Neo-Fundamentalists maintain that they represent an earlier, purer form of Fundamentalism that has been obscured by the militants.

Fundamentalists became very concerned that Falwell was actually promoting a religious unity far beyond that dreamed of by Billy Graham and the New Evangelicals in the 1950s. In his Moral Majority, Falwell claimed that he had founded a nonreligious political organization that would lobby for morality in legislation and politics. Therefore, he did not hesitate to invite Roman Catholics, Jews, Mormons, and other diverse religious groups to work with him. Militant Fundamentalists rightly pointed to the near-impossibility of holding a "nonreligious" crusade for morality, especially when its leaders were all clergy. Inclusion of these groups in the Moral Majority would only lead Bible-believers to accept the validity of their positions.[45] Saying that these efforts were building religious alliances through political activity, Bob Jones III described Falwell's approach to political action as "the ultimate ecumenism."[46]

Falwell and Van Impe were able to cite some genuine grievances. Sometimes militant Fundamentalists were harsh or extreme in their criticism, and some separatists certainly majored on minors. However, the pose of Falwell and Van Impe as reformers trying to call Fundamentalism back to its original position was undermined by their own shifts in theological alliances. Falwell clearly moved from an opposition to the Charismatic movement, for example, to a cooperation with the movement. Liberty University began to accept Charismatic students after Falwell had earlier said it would not do so.[47] Van Impe moved even farther in his associations. Most surprising was his jubilant embrace of Roman Catholicism as a partner not just in moral reform but also in evangelism and discipleship.[48] No appeal to any previous period of Fundamentalist history could support alliances such as these.

It is difficult to see Neo-Fundamentalism as any more than a halfway house to the New Evangelical position. C. T. McIntire observes that Neo-Fundamentalists "tended to blur the distinction between fundamentalist and evangelical."[49] Neo-Fundamentalism's position on ecclesiastical separation—the crucial difference between Fundamentalist and non-Fundamentalist Evangelicalism—is virtually indistinguishable from that of the majority of Evangelicals. Falwell eventually ceased calling himself a Fundamentalist in favor of the name *Evangelical.* He openly affirmed his cooperation with non-Fundamentalist Evangelicals, Charismatics, and Catholics. By the time Falwell invited Billy Graham to speak at the commencement of Liberty University in 1997 (where Graham's grandson was part of the graduating class), there seemed to be no difference at all between the two movements.

Conclusion

By no means are all Evangelicals letting theological drift take place without any protest. We have already mentioned Harold Lindsell's *Battle for the Bible* and his call for the defense of inerrancy. Shortly before his death, Evangelical writer and apologist Francis Schaeffer warned in *The Great Evangelical Disaster* against the increased accommodation of Evangelicalism to worldliness. More recently, John MacArthur echoed Schaeffer's concerns. Likewise, although on a more scholarly level, David Wells warned against theological compromise that threatens the theological and intellectual underpinnings of Evangelicalism.[50] Furthermore, some writers soundly criticized particular doctrinal deviations. MacArthur challenged the Charismatic movement, for example, and both he and R. C. Sproul spoke out against the accommodations Evangelicals are making to Roman Catholicism.[51]

Fundamentalists may read such critiques with great profit, but they should realize that the authors of these books still differ with them over ecclesiastical separation and even points of personal separation. Such writers take a commendable stand against error.

Yet they remain part of a network of organizations and alliances that accepts and promotes tolerance of false teaching and wrong practice. It was part of the Neo-Fundamentalist error to assume that a common opposition to certain dangers provides a basis for unity between Fundamentalist and non-Fundamentalist Evangelicals. But as we have seen, the basis for unity must not be a common opposition to error but a common commitment to biblical truth and biblical practice.

We must observe that the New Evangelicalism and its heirs adopted wrong strategies that led them into error. They thought that they could make a greater impact on the world through what they considered a more intellectually credible presentation of orthodox Christianity. But as John Sanderson points out, liberals and secularists do not reject Christianity because it is poorly presented but because it is *Christian*.[52] They thought they could make greater inroads for the gospel by cooperating with liberals in evangelism. But in doing so they made partners of the very people who were supposed to be the objects of evangelism. They thought that by lowering standards of personal separation they could accommodate and thereby attract the world. But as Jerry Huffman notes, "We cannot rescue a man sinking in quicksand by jumping in with him."[53] Blurring the distinctions that God has set down is never a legitimate means of advancing the Christian faith.

Finally, we should remember that non-Fundamentalist and Fundamentalist Evangelicals are Christian brethren. Therefore, in his opposition to the teachings of the New Evangelical, the Fundamentalist must bear in mind Paul's command to "count him not as an enemy, but admonish him as a brother" (II Thess. 3:15). The goal of separation from the New Evangelicalism is not only purity but also the restoration of Christian brethren. Admittedly, there does not seem to be a high success rate in urging Evangelicals to return to the biblical position concerning separation. But just as obedient Christians must practice biblical separation whatever the circumstances, so they must seek to admonish and win the erring Christian despite the discouragements they may face.

The Charismatic Movement
Chapter 10

Before the 1960s, if you had said someone was "charismatic," you would have meant that he had great charm, magnetism, and popular appeal. In this sense, John F. Kennedy was the charismatic young candidate of the Democratic Party for the presidency in 1960. Since 1960, to call someone "Charismatic" could just as well be taken to mean that he speaks in tongues.

The word *charismatic* comes from the Greek words *charis,* "grace," and *charisma,* "gift." The "Charismatic movement" describes an interdenominational Christian movement, worldwide in scope, that has grown enormously since the 1960s. Its major emphasis is on "spiritual gifts," supernatural gifts said to be bestowed by the Holy Spirit. The most notable of these gifts is an ability to speak in tongues as a sign of the Holy Spirit's blessing. Because of its influence and practices, the Charismatic movement poses serious questions to those who would practice the Bible's teaching concerning personal and especially ecclesiastical separation.

History of the Charismatic Movement

The Charismatic movement emerged from a movement born early in the twentieth century known as Pentecostalism. To understand the Charismatic movement, we must first understand the Pentecostal movement.[1]

The Development of Pentecostalism

Pentecostalism arose out of the nineteenth-century holiness movement, which we mentioned briefly in Chapters 1 and 6. Holiness Christians emphasize the need for a devout, upright life. Methodist holiness Christians teach that the Holy Spirit eliminates the sinful nature in the believer through a second work of grace after conversion. Keswick holiness advocates teach that the power of the Holy Spirit suppresses the sinful nature. Both agree that the Christian can live in victory over conscious sin. This idea of a "second blessing" after salvation led many to search for further spiritual gifts.

Among these searchers was Charles Parham, a holiness preacher who headed a small Bible college in Topeka, Kansas. Parham later reported how on December 31, 1900, a student named Agnes Ozman asked him to lay hands on her and pray that she might receive the Holy Spirit. Parham did so, and as he prayed she suddenly began to speak in another language, allegedly Chinese. This event has traditionally marked the birth of Pentecostalism.

There had been occasional outbreaks of tongues speaking throughout church history before 1900. The Montanists were a group in the early church (active c. A.D. 150-350) characterized by the giving of prophecies and speaking in tongues. Likewise, during a time of intense persecution by the Catholic Church in the 1700s, a group of persecuted French Protestants practiced tongues speaking. Other groups such as the Shakers and the Mormons (American sects) and the Irvingites (a British group) also practiced tongues speaking at various times. These were all isolated incidents, however.[2] The events associated with Parham sparked a movement that has grown and continued to spread to the present.

Others heard Parham teach on the gift of tongues and joined his cause. One of these, a black holiness preacher named William J. Seymour, held a series of meetings in Azusa Street in Los Angeles from 1906 to 1909. Word of the displays of tongues speaking and faith healing soon spread, and crowds thronged to the "Azusa Street Revival." The fame of Azusa Street gave momentum to the young movement. It took the name *Pentecostal* in reference to the filling of the Holy Spirit on the day of Pentecost (Acts 2:4). Pentecostals claim that, as at Pentecost, the sign of the baptism of the Holy Spirit is to speak in tongues.

From these beginnings the movement blossomed. Today there are many Pentecostal bodies. Among the largest are the Church of God in Christ, the Assemblies of God, the United Pentecostal

Church, the Church of God (Cleveland, Tennessee), and the Pentecostal Holiness Church. As the contribution of William Seymour suggests, there has been a large African American contribution to Pentecostalism. An example is the Church of God in Christ, founded by C. H. Mason, who joined the Pentecostal movement after visiting Seymour's Azusa Street meeting. It has become the most important predominantly black Pentecostal group and one of the largest and fastest-growing Pentecostal denominations.

Rise of the Charismatic Movement

The transformation of Pentecostalism into Neo-Pentecostalism—or as it is better known, the Charismatic movement—was the result of several factors. On the one hand, Pentecostals reached out to the mainstream of American religion. But the event that really launched the movement was when the mainstream reached out to Pentecostalism.

The first Pentecostal outreach toward the mainstream was Pentecostal interest in the ecumenical movement. The career of David DuPlessis, a man often called "Mr. Pentecost," illustrates this trend. Born in South Africa in 1905, DuPlessis became a Pentecostal minister after his conversion. In the late 1940s and early 1950s, he made acquaintance with others of his denomination at various worldwide Pentecostal meetings and, as a result, he moved to the United States in 1949. In 1951 he approached the World Council of Churches (WCC) to promote both recognition of Pentecostalism and involvement by Pentecostals in the ecumenical movement. DuPlessis appeared as an observer in many ecumenical meetings, such as the WCC gatherings at Evanston, Illinois (1954), and New Delhi (1961), and the Roman Catholic Vatican Council of the 1960s.

A second outreach was the effort of Oral Roberts to move into the mainstream. An evangelist in the Pentecostal Holiness Church, Roberts became one of the best-known Pentecostal preachers in the nation in the 1950s and 1960s through his tent meetings and television program. Roberts eventually rose to prominence in the Charismatic movement by expanding his ministries to include non-Pentecostals. He did so by founding the nondenominational, but Charismatic, Oral Roberts University (1965) and by joining the United Methodist Church (1968).

A third outreach involved changing the social perception of Pentecostalism. From its beginning, the Pentecostal movement was strongest in rural areas and among the urban blue-collar working classes. This fact created a sort of snobbery against it as a "lower-class" religion. A conscious effort to change this image was the founding of the Full Gospel Business Men's Fellowship International in 1951 by Demos Shakarian. The FGBMFI clearly demonstrated that Pentecostals had appeal among the white-collar workers of the upper middle class. Also, although the FGBMFI was at first composed only of Pentecostals, it is independent of any denomination. Therefore, when the Charismatic movement began to grow, the organization appealed to converts in all denominations.

These activities all contributed to the rise of the Charismatic movement. The event that really sparked the movement, however, came in 1960. Dennis Bennett, pastor of St. Mark's Episcopal Church in Van Nuys, California, "received the gift" and began to speak in tongues. Significantly, Bennett did not leave the Episcopal Church and join a Pentecostal group but remained within his denomination.

Bennett's conversion represented a great shift. Pentecostal teaching began to invade mainstream denominations and became a widespread phenomenon. Tongues speaking spread like wildfire, and Charismatics began to appear among Baptists, Lutherans, Methodists, and even Catholics. The first mass gathering of Pentecostals and Charismatics was held in 1977 in Kansas City. Fifty thousand people attended, representing some fifty million Pentecostals and Charismatics around the world. Fully half of those attending were Roman Catholics.[3]

Much like Fundamentalists after the 1920s, Charismatics began to build their own network of schools, periodicals, and fellowships. They attracted public attention through their efforts at television broadcasting. Oral Roberts's successful program paved the way for these efforts, but it was Charismatic Southern Baptist Pat Robertson who achieved the greatest renown. Starting with just one television station in 1961, Robertson built an enormous television empire. The popularity of his program *The 700 Club* helped create his Christian Broadcasting Network (CBN). CBN in turn helped launch other institutions, such as Regent University. Television success also gave Robertson a platform for political ventures. He ran unsuccessfully for the Republican presidential nomination in 1988. Later he founded the Christian Coalition, a political-action organization that replaced the Moral Majority as the major voice of the religious right. Robertson was but the most visible of a number of Charismatic ministers and "television personalities."

Recent Trends

It is sometimes difficult today to see any distinction between Pentecostalism and the Charismatic movement, but there are differences. Pentecostals have remained in their distinctive denominations. They belong to clearly Pentecostal bodies such as the Pentecostal Holiness Church or the Assemblies of God. Charismatics, on the other hand, generally belong to churches in the major denominations. Normally, Pentecostals insist on speaking in tongues as the mark of the Holy Spirit's baptism, but Charismatics are sometimes open on this question.[4] Historically, Pentecostals have been stricter than Charismatics in personal and ecclesiastical separation. Pentecostal Ray Hughes notes that "one of the most painful concerns among some traditional Pentecostals is the lifestyle of some who profess the baptism in the Spirit. Most of the traditional Pentecostals believe in a 'separated life,' and many of the new Pentecostals do not."[5] As we will see, lack of separation from false teaching and from disobedient Christians is one of the major weaknesses of the Charismatic movement. Despite these differences, the two movements generally cooperate with one another today.

The movements have continued to grow and to develop. The 1980s saw the emergence of what is known as the "third wave" or the "signs and wonders" movement. Just as Pentecostalism was the first wave of the Holy Spirit and the Charismatic movement was the second wave, so the signs and wonders supposedly represent a third wave of spiritual blessing. The third wave appeals to Evangelicals who want to be neither Pentecostal nor Charismatic but seek the same kind of spiritual gifts. Supporters of this position claim that miraculous signs and wonders are necessary to proclaim the gospel. They advocate "power evangelism," in which the preaching of the gospel is accompanied by alleged miracles such as healings and exorcisms of demons. Among the leaders of this third wave were John Wimber and his Vineyard Christian Fellowship.[6] One of the most visible examples of the signs and wonders movement has been the "Toronto blessing," or "laughing revival," which grew out of the Vineyard movement. The mark of the Toronto blessing is the claim that periods of uncontrolled laughter are signs of the Holy Spirit's moving.[7]

Pentecostal and Charismatic growth has been even more spectacular outside the United States. D. B. Barrett reported in 1988 that Pentecostalism and its offshoots numbered 332 million adherents worldwide. Of this number, Barrett said, 176 million were Pentecostals, 123 million were Charismatics, and 28 million belonged to the third wave.[8] Unquestionably Pentecostalism and the Charismatic movement were among the most influential worldwide religious movements of the twentieth century. The question is whether their impact was good or bad.

Fundamentalism and Pentecostalism

Some writers, such as Robert Mapes Anderson and Virginia Brereton, profess to see early Pentecostalism as another form of Fundamentalism.[9] They stress characteristics such as Pentecostalism's emphasis on biblical literalism, opposition to Modernism, belief in premillennialism, and willingness to practice both personal and ecclesiastical separation.

Early Fundamentalists generally opposed the movement, however. Bible commentator G. Campbell Morgan is reputed to have called Pentecostalism "the last vomit of Satan." W. B. Riley likewise opposed Pentecostal teaching and refused to allow Pentecostals to hold membership in the World's Christian Fundamentals

Association.[10] Perhaps part of the Fundamentalist resistance was the lower social status of Pentecostalism and its extremist reputation. Fundamentalists did not want to be identified with these "holy rollers." But the heart of the disagreement was—and remains—Fundamentalist rejection of Pentecostal distinctives.[11]

Fundamentalists protest first against the most prominent Pentecostal teaching, that speaking in tongues is a sign of the baptism of the Holy Spirit. Fundamentalists are usually "cessationists," Christians who believe that some spiritual gifts, such as speaking in tongues and special acts of healing, ceased at the close of the New Testament era.[12] They therefore reject one of the most basic Pentecostal teachings, saying that all believers are baptized by the Spirit (without speaking in tongues) when they are converted.

Even allowing that speaking in tongues is possible, Fundamentalists say that the Pentecostal practice of tongues is not scriptural. For example, in I Corinthians 14:26-32, Paul sets down rules for speaking in tongues in church. There should be no more than two or three people speaking in tongues in a service, and no one should do so if an interpreter is not present. Those who speak should do so in order and not simultaneously. Fundamentalists maintain that these instructions are usually not followed in Pentecostal circles.

A major concern to Fundamentalists is the tendency of some who speak in tongues to consider their utterances a special revelation from God. Fundamentalists (and many other Evangelicals) reject the idea of special revelation apart from the Bible. Paul teaches in II Timothy 3:15-17 that the Scriptures provide *everything* needed for salvation and Christian living. No extra revelation can be binding on the conscience of a believer. Long before the Pentecostal movement ever arose, John Wesley (whom Pentecostals see as one of their forerunners) warned,

> Give no place to a heated imagination. Do not hastily ascribe things to God. Do not easily suppose dreams, voices, impressions, visions, or revelations to be from God. They may be from him; they may be from nature; they may be from the devil. Therefore "believe not every spirit, but try the spirits whether they be of God." Try all things by the written word,

and let all bow down before it. You are in danger of enthusiasm every hour if you depart ever so little from Scripture; yea, or from the plain literal meaning of any text taken in connection with the context. And so you are if you despise or lightly esteem reason, knowledge, or human learning; every one of which is an excellent gift of God, and may serve the noblest purposes.[13]

Finally, Fundamentalists have generally been concerned about an attitude of spiritual superiority that characterizes Pentecostal teaching. There is almost an arrogance to the claim that Pentecostalism has the "full gospel." The implication is that non-Pentecostals have only a partial gospel. Such an idea is unscriptural. Paul told the Colossian believers, "And ye are complete in him, which is the head of all principality and power" (Col. 2:10). The salvation of Christ through the gospel is perfect and complete. Christians should grow in grace (II Pet. 3:18), but this growth is the realizing of what Christ has already granted to the believer. As Paul wrote, "I follow after, if that I may apprehend that for which also I am apprehended of Christ Jesus" (Phil. 3:12).

Yet, despite these differences, at least a few Fundamentalists are willing to regard some issues as matters of interpretation and to suggest a basis for fellowship with conservative Pentecostals. Bob Jones Jr. cites an independent Pentecostal who withdrew from his denomination in protest over its participation in the Charismatic movement and says that he "is as much of a Fundamentalist as I am." Jones goes on to refer to other independent, old-line Pentecostal churches that have withdrawn from the major Pentecostal denominations in protest against the Charismatic movement. He argues that there is a place for fellowship with such believers. Still, he draws the line at accepting teachings such as receiving new revelation, tongues, and the gift of healing. Such teachings go beyond what he sees as the bounds of mere differences of interpretation.[14]

There are many extremes in the Charismatic movement that Fundamentalists reject. Fundamentalists (along with many other Christians) cringed in 1987 when Oral Roberts claimed that God had threatened to take him home if Roberts did not get $8 million by a certain date. The secular media jokingly compared this to a hostage situation with God issuing the ransom demand. Charismatic Jim Bakker and Pentecostal Jimmy Swaggart, both leading televangelists, became enmeshed in sex scandals that made headlines. But defenders of a movement can always claim that extremes are not typical. A key and indisputable difference between Fundamentalism and the Charismatic movement, and those Pentecostals who go along with the Charismatics, is the question of separation. In some cases the point of dispute is personal separation. The worst examples are entertainers and athletes who claim to have had Charismatic experiences of some kind but whose worldly lifestyles hardly "shew forth the praises of him who hath called [them] out of darkness into his marvellous light" (I Pet. 2:9). To be fair, we should note that many Charismatics and Pentecostals uphold biblical standards of personal behavior.

Far more often the problem is ecclesiastical separation. The basis of Christian unity for Charismatics is not so much an agreement on the essential truths of Christianity but rather a shared spiritual "experience." James Richard Monk, for example, cites leading Catholic Charismatic Edward O'Connor: "When the charismatic renewal, after having been confined for decades to the Pentecostal denominations, began to penetrate into the established churches, it naturally tended to create bonds among all those who embraced it. These were not, however, bonds of doctrinal agreement; for it is not the spread of *ideas* about the Holy Spirit that constitutes the Pentecostal movement, but the *experience* of the Spirit's power action."[15]

By no means are all Charismatics and Pentecostals so flexible with doctrine. Ray Hughes, a traditional Pentecostal, says that a common experience cannot build unity where there is no agreement on doctrine. He points out that non-Christians, even Satanists, have spoken in tongues and that therefore the experience of tongues by itself cannot provide a basis for unity.[16] Jack Hayford likewise argues that Christians must agree on the person and work of Christ as Creator, Redeemer, God's Son, and Savior, in addition to spiritual gifts, before they can know true unity. Yet Hayford says that

"biblical unity is discovered not as a resolution of doctrinal differences, but as a revelation of the Living Word—Jesus."[17] W. Dennis
Pederson argues that God "will unify His body through those who
are open to His Spirit," and he urges Charismatics to remain in their
churches in the compromised major denominations.[18]

An example of the dangerous doctrinal breadth of the Charismatic movement is its acceptance of Krister Stendahl. The dean of
Harvard Divinity School in the 1970s and later a bishop in the
Church of Sweden (Lutheran), Stendahl completely accepted rationalist historical criticism of the Bible. He wrote a work arguing
that the Gospel of Matthew was not written by that apostle but by
a much later "school of Matthew."[19] Stendahl also contended that
only I Thessalonians, Galatians, I and II Corinthians, Philippians,
Philemon, and Romans were actually written by Paul.[20] Yet Stendahl
claimed to be a Charismatic baptized by the Holy Spirit, and he was
a featured speaker in Charismatic conferences.[21]

We could cite other examples, such as the doctrinal errors of
Catholic Charismatics who try to reconcile Catholic and Pentecostal teaching.[22] Truly, there can be no spiritual unity where there is
no salvation through the work of the Holy Spirit. But likewise, there
can be no unity of the Spirit where truth is sacrificed. Jesus said of
the Holy Spirit, "When he, the Spirit of truth, is come, he will guide
you into all truth" (John 16:13). When a movement moves to
embrace error, it is not being guided by the Holy Spirit, despite
what its adherents may say.

Conclusion

As we have said, there are many extremes in the Charismatic
movement that give the Fundamentalist pause. Furthermore, we
have seen important doctrinal disagreements between Fundamentalists and Charismatics. These matters alone may give the Fundamentalist sufficient reason to distance himself from the movement.

But the greatest danger of the Charismatic movement lies in its
ecumenicity—its willingness to embrace all sorts of doctrinal
deviations in the name of Christian unity and under the supposed
leading of the Holy Spirit. The Charismatic movement blurs the

division between truth and error and therefore promotes a false unity.

Probably some unregenerate people are being deceived into thinking they are Christians because they have had some kind of Charismatic experience. Many other Charismatics and Pente-costals are genuine Christians, sincere in their desire to serve God. Jesus told the woman of Samaria that "true worshippers shall worship the Father in spirit and in truth: for the Father seeketh such to worship him" (John 4:23). To worship and serve in the power of the Holy Spirit is essential to Christian living, but such worship and service will also always be in truth.

Roman Catholicism
Chapter 11

Before the 1960s, virtually any Protestant in the United States would have thought it stating the obvious to warn Christians to keep their distance from Roman Catholicism. In 1946 noted liberal Protestant Charles Clayton Morrison wrote in *Christian Century,*

> Catholicism is more than a way of salvation. Seen whole, it presents itself as a system of power—a kind of power which no human institution should presume to possess and exercise, a power which is radically incompatible with both Christianity and democracy, and which carries within itself the seeds of corruption. The Roman Church is a monarchical and feudal institution. . . . The hierarchy, with the pope at its head, is the counterpart (or should I say the prototype?) of the fascist or nazist or communist "party" with the dictator at its head.[1]

Today the situation is drastically different. We have looked at several theological systems in the historical order in which they emerged: liberalism, Neo-orthodoxy, the New Evangelicalism, and the Charismatic movement. Roman Catholicism is older than all of these combined, but only in the relatively recent past has there been a general acceptance of Catholics by Evangelicals followed by Evangelical efforts to join hands with Catholics in both political and religious efforts.

The Heart of Catholicism
Origins

Probably one of the most asked—and least answerable—questions in church history is "When did the Roman Catholic Church begin?" Men have offered various ideas, aside from the Catholic claim that it is simply the true church since New Testament times. The Protestant reformers generally held to the papal theory. According to this view, when the popes (bishops of Rome) took the overlordship of the church, they corrupted it into the Roman Catholic Church of today. One question would be with which bishop of Rome this corruption began. Suggestions include Leo the Great (440-61), Gregory the Great (590-604), and Gregory II (715-31). The papacy alone, however, cannot bear the blame for all of the problems of Catholicism.

Another popular idea is the Constantinian theory. When the Roman emperor Constantine embraced Christianity in A.D. 313, he began the process of bringing the pagan masses of the empire into the Christian church. These unregenerate crowds, with their superstitions, transformed and corrupted the church into the Roman Catholic Church. There is an element of truth to this theory, certainly. Making all Roman citizens members of the church introduced greater superstition and unquestionably sped up the process of corruption. Some distinctive Catholic teachings existed before Constantine's time, however, and many other doctrines developed later.

Some hold that the Council of Trent marks the establishment of the Roman Catholic Church. That council, held in three sessions from 1545 to 1563, expressly rejected the teachings of the Protestant Reformation and demanded submission to all teachings required by the Catholic hierarchy. By this decision, this theory holds, the Roman Catholic Church locked itself into a system of false teaching. Again there is much truth to this idea. Trent drew hard lines between Catholicism and Protestantism and forced all who held Protestant ideas either to submit or to leave the church. We should not ignore the fact, though, that the teachings required of all Catholics by Trent had existed in one form or another before the Reformation; they just had not formerly been made official.

Authority and Salvation

Each of these theories contains an element of truth. The Roman Catholic Church is the result of a process of development over a period of centuries. At the same time, its teachings have remained fairly stable since the Reformation. There are many points of difference between Catholicism and biblical Christianity that we could note. As examples, we will focus on just two major issues: the authority of Scripture and the nature of salvation.[2]

The Protestant reformers clearly stated that the Bible alone is the authority in religious matters. The Catholic Church replied that Scripture and tradition are both to be religious authorities. By "tradition" Catholics mean a body of oral teaching given by Christ to the apostles along with the written Scriptures. This oral tradition is the authority for the nonbiblical Catholic teachings rejected by Protestants. Karl Keating, writing to warn Catholics against Fundamentalism, notes that some Catholics looking through the pages of their Bibles "are dismayed to discover there is no clear mention of auricular confession, infant baptism, or the Immaculate Conception in any book from Matthew to Revelation."[3] Later, dealing with the Assumption of Mary (i.e., that Mary was bodily taken to heaven at the end of her life), he writes, "Still, fundamentalists ask, where is the proof from Scripture? Strictly, there is none. It was the Catholic Church that was commissioned by Christ to teach all nations and to teach them infallibly. The mere fact that the Church teaches the doctrine of the Assumption as something definitely true is a guarantee that it *is* true."[4]

As the last quotation from Keating indicates, not only do Catholics view tradition as an authority, they also believe that the church, under the leadership of the popes and bishops, is the only interpreter of what Scripture and tradition actually teach. Edward Panosian notes that the practical effect is not to have two sources of authority, Scripture and tradition, but one authority, the church that interprets Scripture and tradition.[5] In 1870 the First Vatican Council strengthened this idea by declaring that the pope is preserved from all error when pronouncing official church teaching. Pope Pius XII invoked this authority, for example, when he declared in 1950 that all Catholics must believe in the Assumption of Mary.

The doctrine of salvation is another key battleground. The Bible teaches salvation by faith; the Catholic Church teaches salvation by faith and works. In particular, the Protestant reformers declared that a man is justified by faith alone. He is declared righteous by having the righteousness of Christ credited to him. Roman Catholicism teaches that a man is justified by faith and works.

In an effort to build bridges between Catholics and Evangelicals, Alister McGrath says that "some evangelicals continue to insist that the Roman Catholic church officially teaches justification by works, yet that is simply not true"[6] McGrath's observation is partly correct. Catholics do not believe that anyone can be saved without faith. However, they equally believe that no one will be saved without works. Both are necessary in Catholic teaching.

The problem is that Catholicism confuses justification with sanctification. Biblically speaking, in justification the Christian is declared righteous on the basis of Christ's atonement, not on any merit of his own. In the process of sanctification, as a result of his justification, a Christian actually becomes more righteous in thought and action. Catholics, however, say that in justification righteousness is actually poured into the believer so that he really becomes more righteous. Salvation becomes a process in which the Catholic, on the basis of faith, strives to be righteous enough to merit heaven. In other words, instead of being declared righteous, he actually becomes more righteous.

What good works must Catholics perform? Chief among their duties is to receive the sacraments. There are seven of these: baptism, confirmation, holy orders (ordination), matrimony, penance, Eucharist (the Lord's Supper), and anointing of the sick (formerly known as extreme unction or last rites). By participating in these sacraments, Catholics believe they receive grace from God. That grace in turn enables them to perform meritorious works to secure their salvation.

The idea of personal merit is obviously very important to Catholicism, but Catholics claim that this merit is earned by the grace of God. God graciously gives the Catholic the ability to perform good works, and God graciously accepts the good works as sufficient for earning merit, even though humans could actually do nothing truly meritorious before God. But Paul says that "to him that worketh is the reward not reckoned of grace, but of debt" (Rom. 4:4).

Later he says of "the election of grace" that "if by grace, then is it no more of works: otherwise grace is no more grace. But if it be of works, then is it no more grace: otherwise work is no more work" (Rom. 11:6).

In effect, the Catholic Church uplifts human merit at the expense of Christ's merit. For example, in Catholic teaching, Christ's satisfaction for sin is sufficient to pay the penalty for eternal punishment and save a person from hell. It is not sufficient, however, to pay for the "temporal" punishment. Catholics must satisfy the temporal punishment either through performing good works or by suffering in purgatory before entering heaven. By contrast, Paul says, "There is therefore now no condemnation to them which are in Christ Jesus" (Rom. 8:1)—neither eternal nor temporal condemnation.

There are other controversial teachings that we could cite. The glorification of the virgin Mary, the intercession of Mary and the saints for Christians, the idea that in the Mass (celebration of the Eucharist) the body of Christ is actually offered in an "unbloody sacrifice"—all of these teachings clash with those of Scripture. In a sense the root of these problems is the first problem we listed. If Roman Catholicism were bound by the authority of Scripture, instead of binding the Scripture to the church's authority, it would not hold these teachings, for there is no scriptural support for them.

Vatican II and Catholic Change

If these are the views of Roman Catholicism, then why would any Evangelical Christian want closer ties with that church? Part of the reason is undoubtedly the weakening doctrinal stance of the major denominations and many Evangelical and Charismatic churches. Another major reason is an apparent change in Catholicism since the Second Vatican Council (1962-65), commonly called "Vatican II." The popular perception is that in Vatican II the Roman Catholic Church underwent major changes that opened the door to cooperation between Catholics and non-Catholics.

Vatican II did introduce significant changes to the Catholic Church. The council encouraged Bible study and authorized new translation work. It revised the church liturgy and dropped Latin in favor of the common languages of the people. Catholic liberals saw a new openness toward liberalism by the council. Most significantly, the Catholic Church began to call non-Catholics "separated brethren" instead of heretics and claimed that both sides had sinned in the Reformation controversy. The council's decree "Catholic Principles on Ecumenism" encouraged discussions about unity between Catholics and non-Catholics.[7]

Although Vatican II introduced changes into the Roman Catholic Church, what is often missed is that these changes did not affect the questions that have divided Catholics and Protestants since the Reformation. The tone was friendlier, but there was no change on essential points of doctrine. The decree on ecumenism, for example, still teaches, "All those justified by faith through baptism are incorporated into Christ" (sect. 3). The decree calls non-Catholics "separated brethren" but chides many of them who "have not preserved the genuine and total reality of the Eucharist mystery" (sect. 22), that is, who do not believe in the physical presence of Christ's body in the Eucharist or that in the Mass is offered a real sacrifice of Christ's body.[8]

Just how little Catholicism had changed was illustrated some thirty years after Vatican II. In 1994 the Catholic Church published a new catechism summarizing official church teaching, the first such official summary since the Reformation.[9] This catechism, although maintaining the friendly tone of Vatican II, reveals no major change in Catholic doctrine.

On authority, for example, the catechism says that "the Church, to whom the transmission and interpretation of Revelation is entrusted, 'does not derive her certainty about all revealed truths from the holy Scriptures alone. Both Scripture and Tradition must be accepted and honored with equal sentiments of devotion and reverence' " (para. 82). The "interpretation" of this revelation belongs to the church, in particular, "to the bishops in communion with the successor of Peter, the Bishop of Rome" (85).

On the question of justification, the catechism does not differ from the Council of Trent. The catechism, in fact, quotes Trent on this point: "Justification is not only the remission of sins, but also the sanctification and renewal of the interior man" (1989). "Justification is conferred in Baptism, the sacrament of faith" (1992), the catechism says, and "includes the remission of sins, sanctification, and the renewal of the inner man" (2019). Salvation to the Catholic Church is still partly by Christ's merit and partly by human merit: "No one can merit the initial grace which is at the origin of conversion. Moved by the Holy Spirit, we can merit for ourselves and for others all the graces needed to attain eternal life, as well as necessary temporal goods" (2027). Essential to salvation are the church's sacraments: "The Church affirms that for believers the sacraments of the New Covenant are *necessary for salvation*" (1129). In light of such statements, it is clear that the gulf between Rome and biblical Protestantism has not narrowed. Despite the reform of many Catholic practices, the doctrinal divide between Catholicism and Protestantism is as great as it ever was.

Evangelicals and Catholicism

In addition to Catholic endeavors such as Vatican II, other factors have promoted closer ties between Catholics and Evangelical Christians. The Charismatic movement was one such element. As we mentioned in the previous chapter, the "Charismatic renewal" won a large number of followers among Catholics. Undoubtedly, some of these Catholics were genuinely converted. But one effect of the growth of Charismatic Catholicism was to make Catholics and their church seem more acceptable to Protestants. Since Catholics were apparently receiving the same spiritual gifts as Protestants, then Charismatic Protestants saw less reason for distancing themselves from Catholics.

Another factor was what has been called "Evangelical cobelligerence." Alister McGrath says that this idea originated with Francis Schaeffer and was expounded by J. I. Packer. McGrath writes, "Its basic principle can be stated as follows. There is no inconsistency in evangelicals' forming alliances or coalitions with others to address issues on which they can agree. Such a coalition would be temporary in nature and limited in its objectives. It would not commit evangelicals to collaboration on any other issue, nor to any acknowledgement or admission of the correctness or incorrectness of the outlooks of such other groups."[10] The idea is that orthodox Christians may form all sorts of temporary alliances with diverse groups as long as they have some common objective. Such alliances with Catholics are also supported by Vatican II's "Catholic Principles on Ecumenism," which encourages Catholics to work with non-Catholics on behalf of social causes (sect. 12).

There is some validity to this position, but only in a limited way. For example, Catholics, Protestants, and many other diverse groups may belong to organizations such as the Republican or Democratic Party. They may then work together for the nomination or election of certain candidates. But such cooperation is not in a religious organization dedicated to religious goals. When religious issues become the basis of an organization, then the biblical teaching concerning religious fellowship must guide its activities. Religious unity that is not based on the essential truths of Scripture will lead only to the compromise of those truths.

An example of the dangers of Evangelical cobelligerence is the organization known as Promise Keepers. College football coach Bill McCartney, a former Catholic and a member of the Charismatic Vineyard movement, founded Promise Keepers in 1991. This "Christian men's movement" sought to inspire men to be better husbands and fathers. Because they sought to affect all "Christian" men, the Promise Keepers welcomed every person of nominal Christian faith, including Catholics.[11] One report said that a tenth of the men who attended Promise Keepers rallies in 1996 were Catholic. Furthermore, it reported that the organization's board took on its first Catholic member and that it began featuring a Roman Catholic evangelist in its rallies. In 1997 Promise Keepers even revised its doctrinal statement on salvation by altering the phrase "through faith alone" to make it less objectionable to Catholics.[12]

One of the most troubling examples of Protestant accommodation to Catholicism is a document known as "Evangelicals and

Catholics Together," or "ECT" for short. This document was drawn up and signed by a number of Catholics and Evangelicals, led by Richard John Neuhaus, a former Lutheran turned Catholic priest, and Charles Colson, a former member of President Richard Nixon's staff who was converted after his involvement in the Watergate scandal. Several leading Evangelicals endorsed the document, including Charismatic leader Pat Robertson; Bill Bright, leader of Campus Crusade; Mark Noll, professor of history at Wheaton College; and J. I. Packer, theologian and professor at Regent College in Canada. Reaction to ECT was not all positive. A number of Evangelicals, Fundamentalists, and even Roman Catholics criticized the document.[13]

The document presents Evangelicalism and Catholicism as equally valid expressions of the Christian faith. It condemns "proselytizing," attempts to convert Catholics to Evangelical Protestantism or vice versa.[14] The trouble with ECT is that it underestimates the importance of the significant differences between Catholicism and Evangelical Christianity. Although it lists "points of difference" between the two, such as the nature of the church and the authority of Scripture,[15] the document does not consider these points important enough to prevent cooperation between Catholicism and Evangelicalism.

Significantly, ECT does not include salvation or justification in its list of differences. Rather it tries to unite the two sides by stating, "We affirm together that we are justified by grace through faith because of Christ."[16] Such a statement, however, covers over deep differences in doctrine. As we have already seen, Roman Catholics believe that Christ's atonement provides the basis for salvation. Furthermore, they believe that God's grace and faith are necessary for salvation. But they do not believe that Christians are justified by faith *alone* apart from all human merit.[17] Unfortunately, the acceptance of Catholicism represented by ECT is the general tendency of Evangelicalism today. But it is a trend that those who uphold biblical teaching must resist.

Catholicism and Biblical Separation

The biblical response to Roman Catholicism is the same as it is for any form of false teaching: Christians are to resist it, expose its teachings, and refuse to have fellowship with it. Catholic error is in some ways more subtle than that of other systems we have looked at. Liberalism, for example, subtracts from the Scriptures' teachings by discarding doctrines such as the inerrancy of the Bible and the deity and resurrection of Christ. Roman Catholicism, however, adds to the Scriptures' teaching—the authority of Scripture *and* tradition, salvation by faith *and* works. This sort of error is more difficult to detect.

J. Gresham Machen once argued that with all of its serious flaws, Roman Catholicism is not as bad as liberalism: "The Church of Rome may represent a perversion of the Christian religion; but naturalistic liberalism is not Christianity at all."[18] This is probably true, although it is unlikely that Machen saw this fact as a basis for unity between Protestants and Catholics. We do not associate with a movement on the basis that it is not as far from the truth as some other movement. Rather we associate with those persons and movements that actively hold to the truth. Edward Panosian notes, "There is enough gospel in Romanism to save a soul who trusts Jesus Christ alone. However, there is also enough of the poison of false presumption leading to damnation for the soul who accepts the promise that none are lost who die in communion with the institutional church."[19]

The controversy with Catholicism reveals that there is more to the fundamentals of the Faith than the lists of fundamentals that emerged from the Fundamentalist-Modernist controversy. As R. C. Sproul contends in replying to ECT, justification by faith alone is also an essential of the gospel. We should hold to it along with the deity of Christ, the virgin birth, and the other teachings that Fundamentalists defended.[20] We might add that the Fundamentalist's stress on the inerrancy and authority of Scripture should also be stated as the inerrancy and authority of Scripture *alone*. Otherwise, human tradition can open the church to unscriptural teachings such as purgatory and the veneration of Mary.

If the Catholic system comes under the biblical definition of false teaching, what about genuine Christians who belong to the Catholic Church? Alister McGrath tries to reassure Evangelicals who resist cooperation with Roman Catholics because of Catholic teachings such as prayers for the dead and the veneration of Mary. He contends, "This reaction . . . rests on the assumption that individual Roman Catholics accept the authority of all the official teachings of their church. The empirical evidence available suggests that large numbers of them simply do not." He cites widespread Catholic disobedience to the church's pronouncements on contraceptives as an example of how Catholics select what they will believe and what they will reject.[21] He maintains that there is sufficient basis for cooperation between truly converted Catholics and Evangelical Protestants.

Christians, however, are bound not only by the Scriptures' teaching concerning false teaching but also its teaching concerning disobedient brethren. If indeed Roman Catholicism is a system of false teaching, then genuine Christians who are members of that system must obey the Bible's commands concerning separation from false teaching. Panosian observes "that the often-suggested exception of 'a good Christian in the Roman Catholic Church' is a misnomer. Such a person is either ignorant or disobedient—ignorant of what Rome teaches or of what the Bible teaches, or disobedient to what Rome teaches or to what the Bible teaches. None of these conditions fits either a 'good Roman Catholic' or a 'good Christian.' "[22] Christians who refuse to abide by commands to separate from false teaching are themselves walking in disobedience.

But as we have noted elsewhere, we do not treat disobedient brethren the same way we treat false teachers. Our goal in maintaining religious separation from Catholic Christians is to "gain" them, to "provoke" them "unto love and good works." Perhaps we have here another application of Jude 23. Catholic believers we are to "save with fear, pulling them out of the fire," all the while "hating even the garment spotted by the flesh," the false teaching of

Catholicism. It may be that such Christians will not understand or appreciate our position. But as we have repeatedly stressed, our duty is to obey God and leave the consequences to Him.

Afterword

In these few pages we have attempted to understand and to apply the teaching of biblical separation. We have seen that it is a part of the Christian's sanctification to separate from worldliness, from false teaching, and from disobedient Christians. Remember that like the quality of holiness of which it is an expression, separation begins internally. It is an attitude of heart that is demonstrated by outward actions. You do not become holy by practicing separation; you practice separation as a testimony to the change that has taken place in your heart through the power of the Holy Spirit.

We can give you no better exhortation for practicing separation than to determine the lines that Scripture lays down for believers and to resolve by God's grace to abide by His standards. The Christian practicing biblical separation may have to leave a church or perhaps break a friendship in order to obey God's Word. Jesus put all such sacrifices in their proper perspective in the light of eternal values: "Verily I say unto you, There is no man that hath left house, or parents, or brethren, or wife, or children, for the kingdom of God's sake, who shall not receive manifold more in this present time, and in the world to come life everlasting" (Luke 18:29-30).

One of our major goals has been to demonstrate that separation is a biblical teaching, not just the practice of the modern Fundamentalist movement. Nonetheless, you will find that in today's religious scene, Fundamentalism presents the major viable option for those who seek to practice separation. You should seek above all to be biblical, not simply to be part of some movement. But do not let any reluctance to be associated with a movement affect your desire to be obedient to God.

As you seek to practice separation, you will undoubtedly be challenged by many, including other Christians, who argue that your practice is wrong. Some may protest that separation is unloving. Remind them that Jesus said, "If ye love me, keep my commandments" (John 14:15). We must direct our love first toward God, then toward others, and always in obedience to Him. Others may point to the Bible's commands for Christian unity. For them, recall the lesson of Romans 16:17 that the path to Christian unity involves putting away false teaching, not ignoring it. Always keep the *whole* of Scripture in mind.

As we said earlier in the book, we cannot anticipate every situation you may encounter as you attempt to practice biblical separation. We can only help lay out the principles you should follow in those situations. Determine to be obedient in all circumstances, and prayerfully seek God's guidance through His Word. Treasure the counsel of godly men, but always test such counsel by the Scripture. If you have a heart regenerated by the Holy Spirit and dedicated to true holiness and biblical love and if you maintain a devotion to God's Word, you have the foundation for practicing biblical separation in a manner that will both honor and glorify your Lord Jesus Christ.

Notes

Preface

[1]See also, e.g., John Ashbrook, *The New Neutralism II* (Mentor, Ohio: Here I Stand Books, 1992); and Douglas R. McLachlan, *Reclaiming Authentic Fundamentalism* (Independence, Mo.: American Association of Christian Schools, 1993).

[2]See, e.g., Mark Noll, *The Scandal of the Evangelical Mind* (Grand Rapids: Eerdmans, 1994), pp. 47, 52, 140-41, 188.

[3]Edward M. Panosian, "Roman Catholicism: A Philosophy," *Focus on Missions,* Spring 1992, p. [1].

Chapter 1

[1]Rolland McCune, "Separation: An Important Benchmark of True Fundamentalism," *Frontline,* May-June 1993, p. 16.

[2]An example of regarding separation from a brother as part of ecclesiastical separation is Rolland D. McCune, "The Self-Identity of Fundamentalism," *Detroit Baptist Theological Seminary Journal* 1 (1996): 28-32. Examples of treating separation from a brother independently are Douglas R. McLachlan, *Reclaiming Authentic Fundamentalism* (Independence, Mo.: American Association of Christian Schools, 1993), pp. 121-37; and Fred Moritz, *"Be Ye Holy": The Call to Christian Separation* (Greenville, S.C.: Bob Jones University Press, 1994), pp. 47-87. There is merit to both positions. In Chapters 3-5, we will use the three categories, in part because separation from Christian brethren is such a sensitive matter that it merits separate attention.

[3]John R. Rice, *Come Out or Stay In* (Nashville: Thomas Nelson, 1974), pp. 217-35.

[4]Peter Masters, *Stand for the Truth* (London: Sword and Trowel, 1996), pp. 16-20.

[5]Rolland McCune, *Ecclesiastical Separation* (Allen Park, Mich.: Detroit Baptist Theological Seminary, n.d.), pp. 5-6.

[6]See, e.g., Ernest D. Pickering, *The Biblical Doctrine of Separation* (Clarks Summit, Pa.: Baptist Bible College, 1976), pp. 13-14; McCune, "The Self-Identity of Fundamentalism," p. 28.

[7]*Epistle to Diognetus* (trans. J. B. Lightfoot) sect. 5.

[8]Tertullian, *De Spectaculis,* Loeb Classical Library (1960; trans. T. R. Glover) sect. 15.

[9]Ibid., sect. 24.

[10]John Wesley, *A Plain Account of Christian Perfection* (Louisville: Pentecostal Publishing, n.d.), p. 62.

[11]Rousas Rushdoony, *Foundations of Social Order* (Fairfax, Va.: Thoburn Press, 1978), p. 19. Lloyd-Jones makes this same point: "The great concern of the [early church councils] was doctrine: definition of doctrine and denunciation of error and heresy." D. Martyn Lloyd-Jones, "The Basis of Christian Unity," in *Knowing the Times* (Edinburgh: Banner of Truth, 1989), p. 154.

[12]In his excellent study of biblical separation, Ernest Pickering devotes several pages to these various separatist groups. See Ernest Pickering, *Biblical Separation: The Struggle for a Pure Church* (Schaumburg, Ill.: Regular Baptist Press, 1979), pp. 11-42. He is more cautious than many writers in treating these groups, and one cannot deny that they were separatists, whatever else they might have been. But one must be careful not to ignore serious doctrinal deviation simply because a person or group is separatistic; Pickering himself warns against this tendency (p. 29).

[13]*The "Down Grade" Controversy: Collected Materials Which Reveal the Viewpoint of the Late Charles Haddon Spurgeon* (Pasadena, Tex.: Pilgrim Publications, n.d.), p. 66. The document quoted is an editorial from Spurgeon's paper *The Sword and the Trowel* published in October 1880.

[14]McCune, "Separation: An Important Benchmark of True Fundamentalism," p. 15.

Chapter 2

[1]Gary Cohen, for example, points out how Robert O. Ferm resorts to false antitheses in his criticism of separatism in *Cooperative Evangelism: Is Billy Graham Right or Wrong?* (Grand Rapids: Zondervan, 1958). See Gary G. Cohen, *Biblical Separation Defended: A Biblical Critique of Ten New Evangelical Arguments* (Philadelphia: Presbyterian and Reformed, 1966), p. 59. Fred Moritz notes how *Christian Life* magazine in 1956 made a dichotomy between evangelism and contending for the faith. Fred Moritz, *"Be Ye Holy": The Call to Christian Separation* (Greenville, S.C.: Bob Jones University Press, 1994, p. 47.

[2]D. Martyn Lloyd-Jones, "The Basis of Christian Unity," in *Knowing the Times* (Edinburgh: Banner of Truth, 1989), pp. 118-63.

[3]Ibid., p. 122.

[4]Ibid., p. 123.

[5]Ibid., p. 160.

[6]Ibid.

[7]D. Martyn Lloyd-Jones, " 'Consider Your Ways': The Outline of a New Strategy," in *Knowing the Times,* p. 186.

[8]Ibid., p. 187.

[9]Peter Masters, *Stand for the Truth* (London: Sword and Trowel, 1996), p. 31.

[10]Although he was often critical of Fundamentalism, Vernon Grounds offers a good distinction between separation and schism; see Vernon Grounds, "Separation Yes, Schism No," *Eternity,* August 1963, pp. 17-22.

[11]L. Nelson Bell, "On 'Separation,' " *Christianity Today,* 8 October 1971, p. 26.

[12]The other verses are 3:17, 3:19, 6:14, 10:36, 11:27, 12:46, 16:28, and 18:37.

[13]One of Fred Moritz's themes is that evangelism is in fact a major purpose of separation. See Moritz, *"Be Ye Holy,"* pp. 29-30, 47-48, 63-65, 91-92. Masters

points out that this outreach can extend to those ensnared by false teaching: "We may show love to people who are in error by trying to win them to the Truth. . . . we may endeavour to reach them *as outsiders,* but we must never condone and recognize their teaching, for this is a high crime against the Word of God," *Stand for the Truth,* p. 14.

[14]Ronald Nash, *The New Evangelicalism* (Grand Rapids: Zondervan, 1963), p. 96. See also Donald Grey Barnhouse, "One Church," *Eternity,* July 1958, pp. 20-21; and Walter R. Martin, "Love, Doctrine, and Fellowship: How Can We Put Them Together?" *Eternity,* November 1960, pp. 22, 56. Martin does criticize love that "is not accompanied by confession of sound doctrine," but he accuses the "ultra-fundamentalists" of having forgotten "the bounds of Christian love" (p. 56).

[15]Moritz, p. 64.

[16]The ideas discussed from this point in the chapter are examined more fully in Randy Leedy, "The Ethic of Love," *Biblical Viewpoint* 30, no. 1 (1996): 5-14.

[17]Ernest Pickering, *Biblical Separation: The Struggle for a Pure Church* (Schaumburg, Ill.: Regular Baptist Press, 1979), p. 173.

[18]D. G. Hart, *Defending the Faith: J. Gresham Machen and the Crisis of Conservative Protestantism in Modern America* (Baltimore: Johns Hopkins University Press, 1994; Grand Rapids: Baker, 1995), p. 166. Likewise Runia speaks of "an unscriptural perfectionism that looks for the 'pure' church." Klaas Runia, "When Is Separation a Christian Duty?" *Christianity Today,* 7 July 1967, p. 7.

[19]James B. Hunt, "The Faith Journey of Frederick Douglass, 1818-1895," *Christian Scholar's Review* 15 (1986): 235. A contrast to Douglass's situation is that of Richard Allen (1760-1831). He too was born a slave. He was converted while still a slave and later saw his master profess faith in Christ. Allen's master, however, was deeply troubled by slavery, and he made a way for Allen to purchase his freedom.

[20]See Howard Edgar Moore, "The Emergence of Moderate Fundamentalism: John R. Rice and 'The Sword of the Lord' " (Ph.D. diss., George Washington University, 1990), pp. 99-100, 131-32.

[21]See Barry Hankins, *God's Rascal: J. Frank Norris and the Beginnings of Southern Fundamentalism* (Lexington: University Press of Kentucky), pp. 127-30.

[22]Randy Leedy notes that this reversal of love for God with love for man is the "basic problem" of the New Evangelicals. "By failing to love God first and foremost, they misdefine the interests of men, or else ignore them entirely." "The Ethic of Love," p. 12.

Chapter 3

[1]Earl Nutz, "Important Lessons: I John 2," *Biblical Viewpoint* 27, no. 1 (1993): 35.

[2]Fred Moritz, *"Be Ye Holy": The Call to Christian Separation* (Greenville, S.C.: Bob Jones University Press, 1994), pp. 53-54.

[3]Ibid., p. 50.

[4]See, e.g., Elton M. Eenigenburg, "Separatism Is Not Scriptural," *Eternity,* August 1963, p. 20; Donald Grey Barnhouse, "One Church," *Eternity,* July

1958, p. 20; and Walter R. Martin, "When Is Separation Necessary?" *Eternity,* January 1961, p. 30.

[5]Eenigenburg, p. 20; see also Paul Barnett, *The Message of 2 Corinthians: Power in Weakness,* The Bible Speaks Today (Downers Grove, Ill.: Inter-Varsity Press, 1988), pp. 130-31.

[6]Klaas Runia, "When Is Separation a Christian Duty?" *Christianity Today,* 23 June 1967, p. 4.

[7]It is worth noting that Charles Hodge, writing well before modern controversies over separation, thinks it wrong to limit the II Corinthians passage to just idolatry. He writes, "The principle applies to all the enemies of God and children of darkness. It is intimate voluntary association with the wicked that is forbidden." *An Exposition of the Second Epistle to the Corinthians* (1859; reprint, Grand Rapids: Eerdmans, 1950), p. 166.

[8]Chester Tulga, *The Doctrine of Separation in These Times* (Chicago: Conservative Baptist Fellowship, 1952), p. 42.

[9]Ibid., p. 10.

[10]Charles Hodge, *Ephesians,* Crossway Classic Commentaries (Wheaton, Ill.: Crossway Books, 1994), p. 173.

[11]D. Edmond Hiebert, *The Thessalonian Epistles: A Call to Readiness* (Chicago: Moody Press, 1971), p. 67.

[12]See Edward John Carnell, *The Case for Orthodox Theology* (Philadelphia: Westminster Press, 1959), p. 121.

[13]See John W. V. Smith, *The Quest for Holiness and Unity: A Centennial History of the Church of God (Anderson, Indiana)* (Anderson, Ind.: Warner Press, 1980), pp. 194-204.

[14]Ken R. Pulliam, "Christian Standards Are Not Legalism," *Frontline,* September-October 1991, p. 7.

[15]Hiebert, p. 68.

Chapter 4

[1]Douglas R. McLachlan, *Reclaiming Authentic Fundamentalism* (Independence, Mo.: American Association of Christian Schools, 1993), p. 125.

[2]J. Randolph Jaeggli, "Current Cults and Trends" in *The Preacher and His Ministry* (Greenville, S.C.: Bob Jones University Press, 1989), vol. 1, p. [3].

[3]Rolland D. McCune, "Doctrinal Non-Issues in Historic Fundamentalism," *Detroit Baptist Theological Seminary Journal* 2 (1996): 171-85.

[4]F. F. Bruce, *The Epistle to the Galatians: A Commentary on the Greek Text,* The New International Greek Testament Commentary (Grand Rapids: Eerdmans, 1981), p. 81.

[5]J. Gresham Machen, *Machen's Notes on Galatians* (Philadelphia: Presbyterian and Reformed, 1972), p. 47.

[6]Quoted in Bruce, p. 83.

[7]Machen, pp. 49-50.

[8]James Montgomery Boice, "Galatians," in *The Expositor's Bible Commentary,* ed. Frank E. Gaebelein (Grand Rapids: Zondervan, 1976), 10:429.

[9]D. Edmond Hiebert, *The Epistles of John: An Expositional Commentary* (Greenville, S.C.: Bob Jones University Press, 1991), p. 306.

[10]Peter Masters, *Stand for the Truth* (London: Sword and Trowel, 1996), pp. 11-12.

[11]Leon Morris, *The Epistle to the Romans* (Grand Rapids: Eerdmans, 1988), p. 539.

[12]Ireneaus, *Against Heresies,* 1.16.3. Irenaeus also claims that they were followers of the Nicolas who was one of the first deacons chosen by the church at Jerusalem (Acts 6:5), but this claim is disputed.

[13]Sketching a hypothetical picture of complete apostasy, he says that "a member may forsake his church or denomination" in such circumstances but warns, "Before a man leave of his own accord, let him be terribly sure the Lord Himself has removed that church's lampstand." Elton M. Eenigenburg, "Separatism Is Not Scriptural," *Eternity,* August 1963, p. 22.

[14]Klaas Runia, "When Is Separation a Christian Duty?" *Christianity Today,* 23 June 1967, p. 4.

[15]Ronald Nash, *The New Evangelicalism* (Grand Rapids: Zondervan, 1963), p. 94.

[16]Runia, p. 4. Italics his. Some might debate his use of the term *church* with Judaism, but his point is worth noting. Although many converted Jews continued to worship for a time in the synagogues (see, e.g., Acts 13:14-42; 17:1-4, 10, 17; 18:3, 19, 24-26), there was by the end of the first century a clear separation of Christianity from Judaism. This would be an example of withdrawal, although we should acknowledge that the Jews were also expelling the Christians.

[17]See, e.g., Eenigenburg, p. 20.

[18]Read, e.g., the poignant testimony of a Christian led astray by liberalism in John P. Jewell, *The Long Way Home* (Nashville: Nelson, 1982).

Chapter 5

[1]Fred Moritz, *"Be Ye Holy": The Call to Christian Separation* (Greenville, S.C.: Bob Jones University Press, 1994), p. 71.

[2]Edward John Carnell, *The Case for Orthodox Theology* (Philadelphia: Westminster Press, 1959), p. 130.

[3]See Charles Hodge, *Commentary on the First Epistle to the Corinthians* (1857; reprint, Grand Rapids: Eerdmans, 1994), p. 85.

[4]Moritz, p. 76.

[5]Leon Morris, *The First and Second Epistles to the Thessalonians,* The New International Commentary on the New Testament (Grand Rapids: Eerdmans, 1959), p. 251.

[6]For a discussion of the meaning of the word, see D. Edmond Hiebert, *The Thessalonian Epistles: A Call to Readiness* (Chicago: Moody Press, 1971), p. 235.

[7]John R. Rice, *Come Out or Stay In* (Nashville: Thomas Nelson, 1974), pp. 206-10, 224-25; Jack Van Impe, *Heart Disease in Christ's Body* (Royal Oak, Mich.: Jack Van Impe Ministries, 1984), pp. 158-61. Van Impe likewise argues for a narrow interpretation of I Corinthians 5:11 (pp. 156-58).

[8]J. Gresham Machen, *Christianity and Liberalism* (1923; reprint, Grand Rapids: Eerdmans, 1981), p. 50.

[9]Douglas R. McLachlan, *Reclaiming Authentic Fundamentalism* (Independence, Mo.: American Association of Christian Schools, 1993), p. 134.

[10]Donald Grey Barnhouse, "Thanksgiving and Warning," *Eternity,* September 1957, p. 9. Italics in original.

[11]Donald Grey Barnhouse, "One Church," *Eternity,* July 1958, p. 20.

[12]Walter R. Martin, "When Is Separation Necessary?" *Eternity,* January 1961, pp. 30-31.

[13]Ernest Pickering also points out that in I Timothy 1:20 Paul uses the same language for the exclusion of Hymeneus that he uses in I Corinthians 5:5 of the immoral man in Corinth. Since II Timothy 2:17-18 describes Hymeneus's error as saying that the resurrection is already past, this certainly seems to be another case of exclusion of a believer over doctrinal error. Ernest Pickering, *Biblical Separation: The Struggle for a Pure Church* (Schaumburg, Ill.: Regular Baptist Press, 1979), p. 219.

[14]See Rice, pp. 217-35.

[15]Robert Lightner, "A Biblical Perspective on False Doctrine," *Bibliotheca Sacra* 142 (1985): 20-21.

[16]Bob Jones, *Scriptural Separation: "First and Second Degree"* (Greenville, S.C.: Bob Jones University Press, 1971), p. 1.

[17]Rolland McCune, *Ecclesiastical Separation* (Allen Park, Mich.: Detroit Baptist Theological Seminary, n.d.), p. 11.

[18]Ibid., p. 10.

[19]John Ashbrook, *Axioms of Separation* (Mentor, Ohio: Here I Stand Books, n.d.), p. 22. Likewise McLachlan writes, "While Christian separation is an indispensable ingredient in the recipe for an authentic Christian life, it is not the single or only ingredient. No recipe for life is really palatable if it consists of only one ingredient" (p. 139).

Chapter 6

[1]The best introduction to the history of Fundamentalism, particularly for the lay Christian, is David O. Beale, *In Pursuit of Purity: American Fundamentalism Since 1850* (Greenville, S.C.: Unusual Publications, 1986); the book provides a clear narrative overview from a Fundamentalist perspective. An older Fundamentalist work, still helpful on some points, is George Dollar, *A History of Fundamentalism in America* (Greenville, S.C.: Bob Jones University Press, 1973). Useful interpretive studies of Fundamentalism are found in two works by George Marsden: *Fundamentalism and American Culture: The Shaping of Twentieth-Century Evangelicalism, 1870-1925* (New York: Oxford University Press, 1980), and *Understanding Fundamentalism and Evangelicalism* (Grand Rapids: Eerdmans, 1991). A pioneering work on Fundamentalist history still worth noting is Ernest Sandeen, *The Roots of Fundamentalism: British and American Millenarianism, 1800-1930* (Chicago: University of Chicago Press, 1970; Grand Rapids: Baker, 1978). A collection of short biographies of Fundamentalist leaders is C. Allyn Russell, *Voices of American Fundamentalism* (Philadelphia: Westminster, 1976); Russell is sometimes critical of Fundamentalism, however. An interesting broad overview of the movement is John Fea, "Understanding the Changing Facade of Twentieth-Century American Protestant Fundamentalism: Toward a Historical Definition," *Trinity Journal* 15

(1994): 181-99; Fea uses a chronological scheme similar to the one used in this chapter.

[2]This approach is probably best represented by the Fundamentalism Project sponsored by the University of Chicago, which has published several hefty volumes under the direction of Martin Marty and R. Scott Appleby. An introduction to this approach is found in Martin Marty and R. Scott Appleby, *The Glory and the Power: The Fundamentalist Challenge to the Modern World* (Boston: Beacon Press, 1992). Critiques of this approach can be found in D. G. Hart, "Fundamentalism(s) Redux," *Evangelical Studies Bulletin,* Spring 1993, pp. 2-4; and Mark Sidwell, "Defining Fundamentalism: A Question of Theology or Sociology?" *Biblical Viewpoint* 30, no. 2 (1996): 73-83.

[3]I wish to acknowledge my debt to my former teacher Dr. Edward Panosian for helping me to understand this idea of the church's progressive understanding of revealed truth. A brief summary of these ideas is found in Mark Sidwell, "Progressive Illumination in Church History," in *The Providence of God in History,* by Edward M. Panosian, et al. (Greenville, S.C.: Bob Jones University Press, 1996), pp. 37-43.

[4]For a good discussion of the historical place of inerrancy in Christian belief, see John D. Woodbridge, *Biblical Authority* (Grand Rapids: Zondervan, 1982).

[5]For a critique of George Marsden's position on this point, see John D. Woodbridge, "Is Biblical Inerrancy a Fundamentalist Doctrine?" *Bibliotheca Sacra* 142 (1985): 292-305.

[6]See Marsden, *Fundamentalism and American Culture,* pp. 132-35.

[7]See Betty A. DeBerg, *Ungodly Women: Gender and the First Wave of American Fundamentalism* (Minneapolis: Fortress Press, 1990); and Margaret Bendroth, *Fundamentalism and Gender, 1875 to the Present* (New Haven: Yale University Press, 1993). Bendroth is more moderate in her views. For a critique of this position, see Mark Sidwell, review of *Ungodly Women,* by Betty A. DeBerg, and *Fundamentalism and Gender,* by Margaret Bendroth, *Biblical Viewpoint,* 29, no. 2 (1995): 120-22.

[8]Kirsopp Lake, *Religion of Yesterday and Tomorrow* (Boston: Houghton Mifflin, 1925), pp. 61-62.

[9]For an overview of this "establishment," see Timothy L. Smith, *Revivalism and Social Reform in Mid-Nineteenth-Century America* (New York: Abingdon, 1957); and Mark Noll, *A History of Christianity in the United States and Canada* (Grand Rapids: Eerdmans, 1992), pp. 163-90, 219-44, 286-309. David Beale views the Prayer Meeting Revival and related movements such as Britain's '59 Revival as the primary progenitor of Fundamentalism (pp. 13-33).

[10]For an overview of the division of Protestant thought in this period, see Marsden, *Understanding Fundamentalism,* pp. 9-61; Ferenc Morton Szasz, *The Divided Mind of Protestant America, 1880-1930* (University, Ala.: University of Alabama Press, 1982); and Martin E. Marty, *The Irony of It All,* vol. 1, *Modern American Religion* (Chicago: University of Chicago Press, 1986), pp. 208-47.

[11]On the development and impact of premillennialism, see Timothy P. Weber, *Living in the Shadow of the Second Coming: American Premillennialism 1875-1982* (Grand Rapids: Zondervan Publishing House, Academie Books, 1983).

[12]On the history of the Bible conference movement, see Sandeen, pp. 132-61; and Mark Sidwell, "The History of the Winona Lake Bible Conference" (Ph.D. diss., Bob Jones University, 1988), pp. 18-47. The text of Niagara's creed is found in Beale, Appendix A, pp. 375-79.

[13]On the history of Fundamentalist Bible schools, see Virginia Brereton, *Training God's Army: The American Bible School, 1880-1940* (Bloomington: Indiana University Press, 1990).

[14]A rather critical history is C. Norman Kraus, *Dispensationalism in America: Its Rise and Development* (Richmond, Va.: John Knox Press, 1958). A favorable, more theologically oriented work from within the movement is Charles Ryrie, *Dispensationalism* (Chicago: Moody Press, 1995). For an interesting liberal view of dispensationalism, see Marty, *The Irony of It All,* pp. 218-32.

[15]On the influence of holiness teaching on Fundamentalism, see Marsden, *Fundamentalism and American Culture,* pp. 72-101.

[16]On Princeton and its influence, see Mark Noll, ed., *The Princeton Theology: 1812-1921* (Grand Rapids: Baker, 1983).

[17]R. A. Torrey, A. C. Dixon, et al., *The Fundamentals: A Testimony to the Truth,* 4 vols. (1917; reprint, Grand Rapids: Baker, 1988). On the background of the pamphlets, see Gerald L. Priest, "A. C. Dixon, Chicago Liberals, and *The Fundamentals,*" *Detroit Baptist Seminary Journal* 1 (1996): 113-34.

[18]On the Presbyterian struggles, see Beale, pp. 113-51; for a liberal viewpoint on this topic, see Lefferts Loetscher, *The Broadening Church* (Philadelphia: University of Pennsylvania Press, 1954).

[19]There is no satisfactory overall history of the Fundamentalist-Modernist controversy. See the relevant sections in Beale for a survey. For an interesting liberal overview, see Martin E. Marty, *The Noise of Conflict 1919-1941,* vol. 2, *Modern American Religion* (Chicago: University of Chicago Press, 1991), pp. 155-214.

[20]On the WCFA, see Beale, pp. 97-109. On Riley, see William Vance Trollinger, *God's Empire: William Bell Riley and Midwestern Fundamentalism* (Madison: University of Wisconsin Press).

[21]Quoted in Beale, p. 195.

[22]Quoted in Beale, p. 206.

[23]For an overview of the Baptist controversies, see Beale, pp. 173-242, and Dollar, pp. 145-72.

[24]On the history of the BBU, see Robert Delnay, *A History of the Baptist Bible Union* ([Winston-Salem]: Piedmont Bible College, 1974). On Norris, see Barry Hankins's critical but perceptive biography, *God's Rascal: J. Frank Norris and the Beginnings of Southern Fundamentalism* (Lexington: University Press of Kentucky, 1996).

[25]On the Presbyterian controversy, see Bradley J. Longfield, *The Presbytery Controversy: Fundamentalists, Modernists, and Moderates* (New York: Oxford University Press, 1991); also still useful is Edwin H. Rian, *The Presbyterian Conflict* (1940; reprint, Philadelphia: Committee for the Historian of the Orthodox Presbyterian Church, 1992). On Machen, see D. G. Hart, *Defending the Faith: J. Gresham Machen and the Crisis of Conservative Protestantism in Modern America* (Baltimore: Johns Hopkins University Press, 1994; Grand Rapids: Baker, 1995).

[26]Most studies of the Scopes Trial are highly unsympathetic to the Fundamentalist side. Better than most is David Goetz, "The Monkey Trial," *Christian History,* no. 55 (1997): 10-18.

[27]The best overview of this period is Joel Carpenter, *Revive Us Again: The Reawakening of American Fundamentalism* (New York: Oxford University Press, 1997). For a much more critical survey of the same period, see Louis Gasper, *The Fundamentalist Movement 1930-1956* (1963; reprint, Grand Rapids: Baker, 1981). For the rise of independent missions in particular, see the four essays on pp. 29-132 of Joel Carpenter and Wilbert R. Shenk, ed., *Earthen Vessels: American Evangelicals and Foreign Missions, 1880-1980* (Grand Rapids: Eerdmans, 1990).

[28]See William G. McLoughlin, "Is There a Third Force in Christendom?" in *Religion in America,* ed. William G. McLoughlin and Robert N. Bellah (Boston: Houghton Mifflin, 1968), pp. 45-72.

[29]Ernest Pickering, *Biblical Separation: The Struggle for a Pure Church* (Schaumburg, Ill.: Regular Baptist Press, 1979), pp. 104-6. He notes also that this same difference in philosophy marked the organizations that gave rise to the GARBC and CBA, the Baptist Bible Union and the Fundamentalist Fellowship, respectively (pp. 100-102).

[30]Billy Graham, "The Lost Chord of Evangelism," *Christianity Today,* 1 April 1957, p. 26.

[31]On this conference, see Howard Edgar Moore, "The Emergence of Moderate Fundamentalism: John R. Rice and 'The Sword of the Lord' " (Ph.D. diss., George Washington University, 1990), pp. 274-76.

[32]On the split in the CBA, see Beale, pp. 289-301, for a Fundamentalist perspective, and Bruce Shelley, *A History of Conservative Baptists* (Wheaton, Ill.: Conservative Baptist Press, 1971, 1981), pp. 69-102, for the majority perspective.

[33]Fundamentalism since the 1950s is the period least well covered in historical writing. See Beale, pp. 341-72, and Fea, pp. 194-98. Fea, however, is most critical of the leaders and events of this period of Fundamentalist history. An interesting and perceptive personal survey of Fundamentalism in this period is Rolland McCune, "Fundamentalism at the Closing of the Twentieth Century" (Detroit Baptist Seminary, n.d.).

[34]See Bill J. Leonard, "Independent Baptists: From Sectarian Minority to 'Moral Majority,' " *Church History* 56 (1987): 504-17.

[35]Useful discussion of these issues, albeit from a narrow perspective, is found in Daniel L. Turner, *Standing Without Apology: The History of Bob Jones University* (Greenville, S.C.: Bob Jones University Press, 1997), pp. 240-49. Although Turner focuses primarily on how these issues affected Bob Jones University, the background he gives and especially the sources included in his notes (pp. 424-29) are extremely helpful. We will discuss the Charismatic movement in Chapter 10.

[36]Fea, p. 195, cites two sources which number Fundamentalists at between 4 and 4.5 million.

[37]Millard Erickson, *The New Evangelical Theology* (Westwood, N.J.: Revell, 1968), pp. 203-4.

[38]Robert L. Sumner, review of *In Pursuit of Purity: American Fundamentalism Since 1850,* by David O. Beale, *The Biblical Evangelist,* 1 December 1986, pp. 2, 4-5.

[39]Harold O. J. Brown, *Heresies: The Image of Christ in the Mirror of Heresy and Orthodoxy from the Apostles to the Present* (Garden City, N.Y.: Doubleday, 1984), pp. 29-30. He also likens Fundamentalism to heresy in stressing only selected doctrines (p. 30). John W. Sanderson, although more sympathetic to Fundamentalism, makes the same charge of reductionism in "Fundamentalism and Its Critics," *Sunday School Times,* 21 January 1961, p. 66.

[40]Ronald Nash, *The New Evangelicalism* (Grand Rapids: Zondervan, 1963), p. 91.

[41]Fred Moritz, *"Be Ye Holy": The Call to Christian Separation* (Greenville, S.C.: Bob Jones University Press, 1994), p. 97.

[42]See Iain Murray, *The Forgotten Spurgeon* (Edinburgh: Banner of Truth, 1973); R. J. Sheehan, *C. H. Spurgeon and the Modern Church* (London: Grace Publications, 1985); and Lewis A. Drummond, *Spurgeon: Prince of Preachers* (Grand Rapids: Kregel, 1992), pp. 661-716.

[43]See D. Martyn Lloyd-Jones, "The Basis of Christian Unity" and "Evangelical Unity: An Appeal," in *Knowing the Times* (Edinburgh: Banner of Truth, 1989), pp. 118-63, 246-57; and Iain Murray, *David Martyn Lloyd-Jones: The Fight of Faith* (Edinburgh: Banner of Truth, 1990), pp. 425-567. Lloyd-Jones did successfully urge his own church, Westminster Chapel of London, to become independent.

[44]"Christian liberty" was one of the causes, for example, of the division in 1937 between the staunchly Reformed Orthodox Presbyterian Church and the overtly Fundamentalist Bible Presbyterian Church. See George Marsden, "Perspectives on the Division of 1937," in *Pressing Toward the Mark: Essays Commemorating Fifty Years of the Orthodox Presbyterian Church,* ed. Charles G. Dennison and Richard C. Gamble (Philadelphia: Orthodox Presbyterian Church, 1986), pp. 295-328.

[45]Arie den Hartog, "Fundamentalism and Our Reformed Heritage," *The Standard Bearer,* 1 January 1977, p. 159. See also Andrew Sandlin, "The Truncated Vision of Modern Fundamentalism: A Review Essay," *Chalcedon Report,* January 1997, pp. 27-30.

[46]Milton L. Rudnick, *Fundamentalism and the Missouri Synod* (St. Louis: Concordia, 1966), pp. 84-85. It is interesting to note that one of Rudnick's complaints is that some Fundamentalists remain in denominations containing liberals despite the Bible's teaching in Romans 16:17, II Corinthians 6:14-16, Galatians 5:9, and Titus 3:9-11 (p. 85).

[47]David E. Gonnella, "Why I Am Not a Fundamentalist," *The Baptist Challenge,* July 1990, p. 6.

Chapter 7

[1]Quoted in J. H. Merle d'Aubigné, *The Triumph of Truth: A Life of Martin Luther* (Greenville, S.C.: Bob Jones University Press, 1996), p. 327.

[2]Quoted in Justo L. González, *A History of Christian Thought* (Nashville: Abingdon, 1975), p. 313. For a survey of the philosophical background of liberalism, see pp. 290-318.

[3]For a conservative overview of biblical criticism, see David S. Dockery, Kenneth A. Mathews, Robert B. Sloan, ed., *Foundations for Biblical Interpretation* (Nashville: Broadman and Holman, 1994), pp. 187-231, 396-453.

[4]Adolf von Harnack, *What Is Christianity?* trans. Thomas Bailey Saunders (London: Williams and Norgate, 1901); these principles are listed on p. 51 and discussed on pp. 51-77.

[5]A brief history of liberal theology up to the twentieth century is Bernard Ramm, "The Fortunes of Theology from Schleiermacher to Barth and Bultmann," in *Tensions in Contemporary Theology,* ed. Stanley N. Gundry and Alan F. Johnson (Chicago: Moody, 1976), pp. 15-41.

[6]For an overview of the growth of liberalism among American Protestants, see David O. Beale, *In Pursuit of Purity: American Fundamentalism Since 1850* (Greenville, S.C.: Unusual Publications, 1986), pp. 70-86; Ferenc Morton Szasz, *The Divided Mind of Protestant America, 1880-1930* (University, Ala.: University of Alabama Press, 1982), pp. 1-55; and Martin E. Marty, *The Irony of It All,* vol. 1, *Modern American Religion* (Chicago: University of Chicago Press, 1986), pp. 15-43. A standard liberal work on the topic is Kenneth Cauthen, *The Impact of American Religious Liberalism,* 2nd ed. (Washington, D.C.: University Press of America, 1983).

[7]See Gerald L. Priest, "A. C. Dixon, Chicago Liberals, and *The Fundamentals," Detroit Baptist Seminary Journal* 1 (1996): 113-34.

[8]Harry Emerson Fosdick, *A Guide to Understanding the Bible* (New York: Harper and Brothers, 1938).

[9]Rauschenbusch summarizes his views in *A Theology for the Social Gospel* (New York: Macmillan, 1917).

[10]H. Richard Niebuhr, *The Kingdom of God in America* (1935; reprint, Hamden, Conn.: Shoe String Press, 1956), p. 193.

[11]For a survey of the various schools of modern theology, see David L. Smith, *A Handbook of Contemporary Theology* (Wheaton, Ill.: BridgePoint, 1992); William Hordern, *A Layman's Guide to Protestant Theology,* rev. ed. (New York: Macmillan, 1968); and Gundry and Johnson, *Tensions in Contemporary Theology.* Radical theologies are discussed, from a radical point of view, in John A. T. Robinson, *Honest to God* (Philadelphia: Westminster, 1963). In many ways, the best critique of liberalism is still J. Gresham Machen, *Christianity and Liberalism* (1923; reprint, Grand Rapids: Eerdmans, 1981).

[12]A good introductory critique of postmodernism is D. A. Carson, "Evangelizing Postmoderns," *The Gospel Witness,* 17 April 1997, pp. 1-10.

[13]*Proslogion* (trans. Sidney Norton Deane), Chap. 1.

[14]For an example of liberalism's continued rejection of orthodox Christianity, see John Shelby Spong, *Rescuing the Bible from Fundamentalism* (San Francisco: Harper, 1991), a best-selling popular summary of modern liberal views of the Bible.

[15]Machen, p. 160.

Chapter 8

[1]William Hordern, *The Case for a New Reformation Theology* (Philadelphia: Westminster Press, 1959), p. 161.

[2]Ibid., p. 17.

[3]The best introduction to Neo-orthodoxy from within the movement is Hordern's *Case for a New Reformation Theology* (Philadelphia: Westminster Press, 1959). The best critique of Neo-orthodoxy is probably Cornelius Van Til, *The New Modernism: An Appraisal of the Theology of Barth and Brunner,* 3rd ed. (N.p.: Presbyterian and Reformed, 1973); it is, however, a somewhat difficult work to read. A good popular-level critique is Charles Caldwell Ryrie, *Neo-Orthodoxy* (Chicago: Moody Press, 1956). See also Robert L. Reymond, *Introductory Studies in Contemporary Theology* (Philadelphia: Presbyterian and Reformed, 1968), pp. 73-153.

[4]Barth's own writings are enormously complex. Perhaps the most accessible works by Barth (which are not a systematic review of his views, however) are *Evangelical Theology: An Introduction,* trans. Grover Foley (New York: Holt, Rinehart and Winston, 1963); and *Dogmatics in Outline,* trans. G. T. Thompson (London: SCM Press, 1949).

[5]Donald Grey Barnhouse, "An Interview with Karl Barth," *Eternity,* April 1984, p. 20. This article is a reprint of the original interview. The text reads "more that appeared" in the third paragraph of this reprint, but this appears to be a typographical error and has been amended.

[6]Bernard Ramm, *After Fundamentalism: The Future of Evangelical Theology* (San Francisco: Harper and Row, 1983), pp. 76-79.

[7]See, e.g., Van Til, pp. 405-7, 418-20.

[8]*Dogmatics in Outline,* p. 93.

[9]A typical, if early, statement of Brunner's views is *The Mediator,* trans. Olive Wyon (New York: Macmillan, 1934).

[10]Hordern, pp. 68-69.

[11]The most readable introduction to Reinhold Niebuhr is his memoir *Leaves from the Notebook of a Tamed Cynic* (San Francisco: Harper and Row, 1929); for a sample of his more substantial works, see *An Interpretation of Christian Ethics* (New York: Harper and Brothers, 1935). For important (though by no means easy) works of H. Richard Niebuhr, see *The Kingdom of God in America* (1935; reprint, Hamden, Conn.: Shoe String Press, 1956); and *Christ and Culture* (New York: Harper, 1951).

[12]Ryrie, p. 12.

[13]Charles W. Kegley and Robert W. Bretall, ed., *Reinhold Niebuhr: His Religious, Social, and Political Thought* (New York: Macmillan, 1956), p. 11. In fairness to Niebuhr, we should note that he is here criticizing the liberals' view of sin, saying that they excuse their denial of human sinfulness by rejecting the story of Adam. Niebuhr does not believe in the story of Adam either, but he affirms human sinfulness.

[14]Reinhold Niebuhr, *Beyond Tragedy* (New York: Charles Scribner's Sons, 1937), p. 30.

[15]Probably the most famous works by Bonhoeffer are *The Cost of Discipleship,* trans. R. H. Fuller (New York: Macmillan, 1959); and *Letters and*

Papers from Prison, ed. Eberhard Bethge, rev. ed. (New York: Macmillan, 1967).

[16]Hordern, p. 62.

[17]Ryrie, p. 62.

[18]Bonhoeffer, *The Cost of Discipleship,* p. 36.

[19]Van Til, p. 2.

[20]Alan Cairns, *Apostles of Error* (Greenville, S.C.: Faith Presbyterian Church, 1989), p. [11].

[21]Ibid., p. [12].

[22]Walter R. Martin, "Love, Doctrine, and Fellowship: How Can We Put Them Together?" *Eternity,* November 1960, p. 22.

[23]See John D. Woodbridge, "A Neoorthodox Historiography Under Siege," *Bibliotheca Sacra* 142 (1985): 3-15; and "The Rogers and McKim Proposal in the Balance," *Bibliotheca Sacra* 142 (1985): 99-113. Rogers and McKim present their view of the history of inerrancy in *The Authority and Interpretation of the Bible: An Historical Approach* (San Francisco: Harper and Row, 1979).

[24]Donald G. Bloesch, *The Future of Evangelical Christianity: A Call for Unity amid Diversity* (Garden City, N.Y.: Doubleday, 1983), p. 165. Some of his criticisms of Neo-orthodoxy are found on p. 48. Bloesch identifies the school at which he teaches, University of Dubuque Theological Seminary, as one of the few schools still reflecting "motifs associated with neo-orthodoxy" (p. 48). He lists numerous mainline and Evangelical theologians, denominations, periodicals, and publishing houses that he says "maintain the salient emphases of neo-orthodoxy" (pp. 46-47).

[25]Cairns, pp. [12-13], warns about the influence of Neo-orthodox ideas in even "Fundamentalist and Bible-believing churches." He is particularly concerned with faith being based on a decision or series of decisions "rather than on the Person and work of the Lord Jesus Christ."

Chapter 9

[1]For a brief history of the use of the word *evangelical,* see Alister McGrath, *Evangelicalism and the Future of Christianity* (Downers Grove, Ill.: InterVarsity Press, 1995), pp. 19-23.

[2]On the definition of Evangelicalism, see Grant Wacker, *Augustus H. Strong and the Dilemma of Historical Consciousness* (Macon: Mercer University Press, 1985), p. 17; David Bebbington, *Evangelicalism in Modern Britain* (Grand Rapids: Baker, 1989), pp. 4-17; and Harold John Ockenga, "Resurgent Evangelical Leadership," *Christianity Today,* 10 October 1960, p. 11.

[3]John W. Sanderson, "Neo-Evangelicalism and Its Critics," *Sunday School Times,* 28 January 1961, p. 82.

[4]David O. Beale, *In Pursuit of Purity: American Fundamentalism Since 1850* (Greenville, S.C.: Unusual Publications, 1986), p. 270. Beale is actually describing with this phrase the popular usage of *New Evangelical,* but the meaning is the same.

[5]Ibid., pp. 261, 267.

[6]Joel Carpenter, *Revive Us Again: The Reawakening of American Fundamentalism* (New York: Oxford University Press, 1997), pp. 195-204. We should note that Carpenter uses Wilbur Smith as his example of a reformer who desired

to "strengthen" Fundamentalism; however, Smith actually had many sympathies to the "revising" approach.

[7]There is no authoritative history of the New Evangelical movement. The closest to an overall history is George Marsden, *Reforming Fundamentalism: Fuller Seminary and the New Evangelicalism* (Grand Rapids: Eerdmans, 1987); it is obviously narrow in its focus. See also George Marsden, *Understanding Fundamentalism and Evangelicalism* (Grand Rapids: Eerdmans, 1991), pp. 62-82. An early apologetic for the movement, highly critical of Fundamentalism, is Ronald Nash, *The New Evangelicalism* (Grand Rapids: Zondervan, 1963). The best of the Fundamentalist critiques of the New Evangelicalism is Ernest Pickering, *The Tragedy of Compromise: The Origin and Impact of the New Evangelicalism* (Greenville, S.C.: Bob Jones University Press, 1994). Also very useful is John Ashbrook, *The New Neutralism II* ([Mentor, Ohio]: Here I Stand Books, 1992); it is a sequel to an earlier critique by his father.

[8]The points in the following paragraphs, unless otherwise indicated, are from Harold J. Ockenga, "Foreword" to *The Battle for the Bible* by Harold Lindsell (Grand Rapids: Zondervan, 1976), pp. [11-12].

[9]See "Is Evangelical Theology Changing?" *Christian Life,* March 1956, p. 19.

[10]Bob Jones, *Cornbread and Caviar: Reminiscences and Reflections* (Greenville, S.C.: Bob Jones University Press, 1985), p. 104.

[11]Sanderson, "Neo-Evangelicalism and Its Critics," p. 82.

[12]"Harold John Ockenga's Press Release on 'The New Evangelicalism,' " Appendix B in Fred Moritz, *"Be Ye Holy": The Call to Christian Separation* (Greenville, S.C.: Bob Jones University Press, 1994), p. 118.

[13]Carl F. H. Henry, *The Uneasy Conscience of Modern Fundamentalism* (Grand Rapids: Eerdmans, 1947), p. 27.

[14]Robert Lon Horton, "The Christian's Role in Society," *Biblical Viewpoint* 15 (1981): 130-37; this article is an abstract of his dissertation. Examples of Evangelical writings that take this approach are Ronald J. Sider, ed., *The Chicago Declaration* (Carol Stream, Ill.: Creation House, 1974); David O. Moberg, *The Great Reversal: Evangelism Versus Social Concern* (Philadelphia: Lippincott, 1972); and Ronald J. Sider, *Rich Christians in an Age of Hunger* (New York: Paulist Press, 1977). Senator Mark Hatfield, an Evangelical social activist, says that to preach redemption without a stress on social action is to "preach only half the gospel." Mark Hatfield, *Conflict and Conscience* (Waco, Tex.: Word, 1971), p. 25.

[15]"Ockenga Press Release," p. 119.

[16]The standard biography of Graham is William C. Martin, *Prophet with Honor: The Billy Graham Story* (New York: Morrow, 1991). Also interesting, though obviously very favorable, is Billy Graham, *Just As I Am: The Autobiography of Billy Graham* (Grand Rapids: Zondervan, 1997).

[17]"Ockenga Press Release," p. 119.

[18]Millard Erickson, *The New Evangelical Theology* (Westwood, N.J.: Revell, 1968), p. 212.

[19]Robert O. Ferm, *Cooperative Evangelism: Is Billy Graham Right or Wrong?* (Grand Rapids: Zondervan, 1958). For responses to Ferm's work, see Gary G. Cohen, *Biblical Separation Defended: A Biblical Critique of Ten New Evangelical Arguments* (Philadelphia: Presbyterian and Reformed, 1966); and

John R. Rice, *Earnestly Contending for the Faith* (Murfreesboro, Tenn.: Sword of the Lord, 1965), pp. 249-309.

[20]Erickson, pp. 198-99.

[21]"Is Evangelical Theology Changing?" pp. 18-19.

[22]Lindsell, pp. 106-21.

[23]Richard Quebedeaux, *The Young Evangelicals: Revolution in Orthodoxy* (New York: Harper and Row, 1974); and *The Worldly Evangelicals* (New York: Harper and Row, 1978).

[24]See *The Young Evangelicals,* pp. 37, 39; and *The Worldly Evangelicals,* p. 100.

[25]See *The Young Evangelicals,* p. 106; and *The Worldly Evangelicals,* pp. 16, 17, 119, 128-30.

[26]James Davison Hunter, *Evangelicalism: The Coming Generation* (Chicago: University of Chicago Press, 1987). He lists the sixteen participating schools on p. 9.

[27]Ibid., p. 24.

[28]Ibid., p. 36.

[29]Ibid., p. 59.

[30]Ibid., pp. 174-75.

[31]See "Passing It On: Will Our Kids Recognize Our Faith?" *World,* 11 March 1989, pp. 5-6.

[32]See Clark H. Pinnock, *A Defense of Biblical Infallibility* (Philadelphia: Presbyterian and Reformed, 1967); and *Biblical Revelation: The Foundation of Christian Theology* (Chicago: Moody, 1971).

[33]See Rex A. Koivisto, "Clark Pinnock and Inerrancy: A Change in Truth Theory?" *Journal of the Evangelical Theological Society* 24 (1981): 139-51. Pinnock replied to this article but admitted many of the charges. Clark Pinnock, "A Response to Rex A. Koivisto," *Journal of the Evangelical Theological Society* 24 (1981): 153-55.

[34]Clark H. Pinnock, "The Destruction of the Finally Impenitent," *Criswell Theological Review* 4 (1990): 243-59.

[35]Millard Erickson, *The Evangelical Left: Encountering Postconservative Evangelical Theology* (Grand Rapids: Baker, 1997), pp. 101-2.

[36]Quoted in Robert E. Kofahl, "Billy Graham Believes Catholic Doctrine of Salvation Without Bible, Gospel, or Name of Christ," *Foundation,* May-June 1997, p. 22. For further discussion of the growth of this teaching among Evangelicals, see Dennis Okholm and Timothy Phillips, ed., *More Than One Way?: Four Views on Salvation in a Pluralistic World* (Grand Rapids: Zondervan, 1995).

[37]Douglas Sweeney notes how the early New Evangelicals were similar to the Fundamentalists in doctrine and outlook, arguing in part that they were more separatist than later Evangelicals. See Douglas Sweeney, "Fundamentalism and the Neo-Evangelicals," *Fides et Historia* 24, no. 1 (1992): 81-96.

[38]Earle Cairns, *Christianity Through the Centuries,* 3rd ed. (Grand Rapids: Zondervan, 1996), p. 485.

[39]Bob Jones, "Pseudo-fundamentalists: The New Breed in Sheep's Clothing," *Faith for the Family,* January 1978, pp. 7, 16. Jones says that the term

Pseudo-Fundamentalism was apparently coined by Virginia Fundamentalist Rod Bell.

[40]See George Marsden, *Understanding Fundamentalism and Evangelicalism* (Grand Rapids: Eerdmans, 1991), pp. 76-81; and C. T. McIntire, "Fundamentalism" in *Evangelical Dictionary of Theology,* ed. Walter Elwell (Grand Rapids: Baker, 1984), pp. 433-36. The terminology is not always exact. Jack Van Impe, for example, accuses the militant Fundamentalists of being "neo-fundamentalist" because they represent, he claims, a change from historic Fundamentalism. Jack Van Impe, *Heart Disease in Christ's Body* (Royal Oak, Mich.: Jack Van Impe Ministries, 1984), pp. 25-26. When Fundamentalists began to use the term *Pseudo-Fundamentalism,* some of the Neo-Fundamentalists retorted that the militants were the "Pseudo-Fundamentalists." See Ed Dobson and Ed Hindson, "Who Are the 'Real' Pseudo-Fundamentalists?" *Fundamentalist Journal,* June 1983, pp. 10-11; and Daniel R. Mitchell, "The Siege-Mentality of Pseudo-Fundamentalism" *Fundamentalist Journal,* February 1987, pp. 59.

[41]The basic position of Neo-Fundamentalism is set out in Jerry Falwell, Ed Dobson, and Ed Hindson, *The Fundamentalist Phenomenon: The Resurgence of Conservative Christianity* (Garden City, N.Y.: Doubleday-Galilee, 1981); and Edward Dobson, *In Search of Unity: An Appeal to Fundamentalists and Evangelicals* (Nashville: Thomas Nelson, 1985). Also numerous articles in Falwell's periodical *The Fundamentalist Journal* (published 1982-89) set forth the Neo-Fundamentalist position.

[42]Falwell, et al., *The Fundamentalist Phenomenon,* pp. 24-25.

[43]Ibid., pp. 139-40, 158-59; Dobson, *In Search of Unity,* pp. 63-64.

[44]Falwell, et al., *The Fundamentalist Phenomenon,* pp. 167-72, 221-23; Dobson, *In Search of Unity,* pp. 136-39.

[45]For a sample of Fundamentalist objections to the Moral Majority, see Bob Jones III, "The Moral Majority," *Faith for the Family,* September 1980, pp. 3, 27-28.

[46]Bob Jones III, "The Ultimate Ecumenism," *Faith for the Family,* September 1985, pp. 3, 9-10.

[47]Falwell states his opposition to the Charismatic movement and to having Charismatic students at Liberty in "Open Letter from Jerry Falwell," *Journal Champion,* 18 August 1978, p. 2.

[48]Fundamentalist reports of Van Impe's sympathy to Catholicism are found in "The Capitulation of Dr. Jack Van Impe to Roman Catholicism and the One World Ecumenical Movement," *Fundamentalist Digest,* July-August 1995, pp. 7-17; and Frank McClelland, "Van Impe's TV Attack on Dr. Paisley," *Revivalist,* November 1995, pp. 3-4.

[49]McIntire, p. 435.

[50]Francis A. Schaeffer, *The Great Evangelical Disaster* (Westchester, Ill.: Crossway, 1984); John MacArthur, *Ashamed of the Gospel: When the Church Becomes Like the World* (Wheaton, Ill.: Crossway, 1993); David F. Wells, *No Place for Truth, or, Whatever Happened to Evangelical Theology?* (Grand Rapids: Eerdmans, 1992); David F. Wells, *God in the Wasteland: The Reality of Truth in a World of Fading Dreams* (Grand Rapids: Eerdmans, 1994).

[51]For criticism of the Charismatic movement, see John MacArthur, *Charismatic Chaos* (Grand Rapids: Zondervan, 1992). For protests against accommo-

dation to Catholicism, see John MacArthur, *Reckless Faith: When the Church Loses Its Will to Discern* (Wheaton, Ill.: Crossway, 1994), pp. 119-52; and R. C. Sproul, *Faith Alone: The Evangelical Doctrine of Justification* (Grand Rapids: Baker, 1995).

[52]John W. Sanderson, "Purity of Testimony—or Opportunity?" *Sunday School Times*, 11 February 1961, p. 111.

[53]Jerry Huffman, "Separation—The Big 'S' Word," *Frontline*, January-February 1992, p. 5.

Chapter 10

[1]The most useful work on the history of Pentecostalism is Stanley M. Burgess and Gary B. McGee, ed., *Dictionary of the Pentecostal and Charismatic Movements* (Grand Rapids: Zondervan Publishing House, Regency Reference Library, 1988). Also helpful are Robert Mapes Anderson, *Vision of the Disinherited: The Making of American Pentecostalism* (New York: Oxford University Press, 1979); Vinson Synan, *The Holiness-Pentecostal Movement in the United States* (Grand Rapids: Eerdmans, 1971); and Donald W. Dayton, *Theological Roots of Pentecostalism* (Metuchen, N.J.: Scarecrow, 1987). We should note that the history of Pentecostalism presented in this book follows the traditional outline of events. However, as the writers cited here and elsewhere note, the actual history is much more complex. Even these authors disagree with each other on many points, such as the relative influence of Keswick and Methodist holiness teaching upon Pentecostalism. Some of the disputed points about Pentecostal history are examined in Joe Creech, "Visions of Glory: The Place of the Azusa Street Revival in Pentecostal History," *Church History* 65 (1996): 405-24.

[2]For a critical but extremely helpful survey of tongues speaking in history, see Victor Budgen, *The Charismatics and the Word of God* (Welwyn, England: Evangelical Press, 1985), pp. 113-99.

[3]H. V. Synan, "Kansas City Conference," in *Dictionary of the Pentecostal and Charismatic Movements*, p. 515.

[4]Ray Hughes of the Church of God (Cleveland, Tennessee) cites the question of speaking in tongues as a major distinction between Pentecostals and Charismatics. He says that Pentecostals believe that tongues is the "normative experience" for the baptism of the Holy Spirit whereas Charismatics do not. Ray H. Hughes, "A Traditional Pentecostal Looks at the New Pentecostals," *Christianity Today*, 7 June 1974, pp. 7-8. Kenneth Kantzer notes the results of a *Christianity Today*/Gallup survey that fewer than a fifth of professing Charismatics claim to have spoken in tongues. Kantzer notes also that Pentecostal leaders admit that only half to two-thirds of the members of their denominations say they have spoken in tongues, but it is still a much higher percentage among Pentecostals. Kenneth Kantzer, "The Charismatics Among Us," *Christianity Today*, 22 February 1980, pp. 25-26.

[5]Hughes, p. 10.

[6]See C. Peter Wagner, *The Third Wave of the Holy Spirit* (Ann Arbor: Vine Books, 1988). For a critique of the third wave, see John MacArthur, *Charismatic Chaos* (Grand Rapids: Zondervan, 1992), pp. 128-51.

[7]The name of the movement derives from the fact that it originated in a Vineyard congregation in Toronto. For a sympathetic introduction to the

Toronto blessing, along with some mild criticisms, see B. J. Oropeza, *A Time to Laugh: The Holy Laughter Phenomenon Examined* (Peabody, Mass.: Hendrickson, 1995). For a pointed and thorough critique, see Eric Wright, *Strange Fire? Assessing the Vineyard Movement and the Toronto Blessing* (Welwyn, England: Evangelical Press), 1996. For an interesting, narrowly focused critique of the laughing revival, see John Hannah, "Jonathan Edwards, the Toronto Blessing, and the Spiritual Gifts: Are the Extraordinary Ones Actually the Ordinary Ones?" *Trinity Journal* 17 (1996): 167-89.

[8]D. B. Barrett, "Statistics, Global," in *Dictionary of the Pentecostal and Charismatic Movements,* p. 811.

[9]Anderson, pp. 5-6; Virginia Brereton, *Training God's Army: The American Bible School, 1880-1940* (Bloomington: Indiana University Press, 1990), pp. 166-69.

[10]A good overview of Fundamentalist-Pentecostal relations, from a Pentecostal point of view, is H. V. Synan, "Fundamentalism," in *Dictionary of the Pentecostal and Charismatic Movements,* pp. 324-27.

[11]Perhaps the best, and certainly the most readable, critique of Pentecostalism and the Charismatic movement is MacArthur's *Charismatic Chaos.* Also very helpful is Budgen's *Charismatics and the Word of God.* Critiques from an avowedly Fundamentalist position are Ernest Pickering, *Charismatic Confusion* (Schaumburg, Ill.: Regular Baptist Press, 1980); and two works by O. Talmadge Spence, *Charismatism, Awakening or Apostasy?* (Greenville, S.C.: Bob Jones University Press, 1978), and *Pentecostalism: Purity or Peril?* (Greenville, S.C.: Unusual Publications, 1989). Spence's critiques are particularly interesting in that they are written from a Pentecostal perspective.

[12]For a defense of the idea of the cessation of these spiritual gifts, see Benjamin B. Warfield, *Counterfeit Miracles* (1918; reprint, London: Banner of Truth, 1972).

[13]John Wesley, *A Plain Account of Christian Perfection* (Louisville: Pentecostal Publishing, n.d.), pp. 46-47.

[14]Bob Jones, *Cornbread and Caviar: Reminiscences and Reflections* (Greenville, S.C.: Bob Jones University Press, 1985), pp. 181-82. For further discussion of Jones's distinction between old-line Pentecostalism and the Charismatic movement, see Daniel L. Turner, *Standing Without Apology: The History of Bob Jones University* (Greenville, S.C.: Bob Jones University Press, 1997), pp. 242-43.

[15]Edward O'Connor, *Pentecost in the Modern World* (Notre Dame, Ind.: Ave Maria Press, Charismatic Renewal Books, 1972), p. 33, cited in James Richard Monk, "Bases of Neo-Pentecostal Ecumenicity" (Th.M. thesis, Dallas Theological Seminary, 1980), p. 55; italics in original. Monk argues that a shared spiritual experience is the basis of unity in Charismatic and Pentecostal circles; see especially his discussion on pp. 54-56.

[16]Hughes, p. 8.

[17]Jack Hayford, "No One Like Jesus," *Charisma and Christian Life,* December 1991, pp. 53-62. The quotation comes from p. 54.

[18]W. Dennis Pederson, "A Time to Mend," *Christian Life,* April 1984, pp. 42, 48.

[19]Krister Stendahl, *The School of St. Matthew* (Philadelphia: Fortress, 1968).

[20]Krister Stendahl, *Paul Among the Jews* (Philadelphia: Fortress, 1976), p. 127.

[21]See, e.g., Krister Stendahl, "The Charismatic Movement and the New Testament," in *What the Spirit is Saying to the Churches,* ed. Theodore Runyon, ed. (New York: Hawthorn, 1975), pp. 19-28. Stendahl gave this address at the Minister's Week at Emory University in 1974, where he appeared on the program with Oral Roberts and David du Plessis, among others.

[22]See Hughes, pp. 9-10, for a summary of how Catholics resolve differences between Pentecostal and Roman Catholic theology.

Chapter 11

[1]Charles Clayton Morrison, "Roman Catholicism and Protestantism," *Christian Century,* 8 May 1946, p. 585.

[2]Probably the best popular critique of Catholicism from an Evangelical point of view is James G. McCarthy, *The Gospel According to Rome: Comparing Catholic Tradition and the Word of God* (Eugene, Ore.: Harvest House, 1995). McCarthy's book is balanced in its language and focuses mainly on doctrinal disagreements between Catholicism and the Scripture. McCarthy's use of the 1994 *Catechism of the Catholic Church* makes his work one of the most up-to-date. Norman L. Geisler and Ralph E. MacKenzie, *Roman Catholics and Evangelicals: Agreements and Disagreements* (Grand Rapids: Baker, 1995) is also a very good summary of the differences between Catholicism and Protestantism, but the authors are eager to find grounds of agreement and cooperation between Catholics and Evangelicals. An older work, but still useful, particularly on the historical background of Catholicism, is David Schaff, *Our Fathers Faith and Ours: A Comparison Between Protestantism and Romanism.* 2nd ed. (New York: G. P. Putnam's Sons, 1928).

[3]Karl Keating, *Catholicism and Fundamentalism: The Attack on "Romanism" by "Bible Christians"* (San Francisco: Ignatius Press, 1988), p. 84.

[4]Ibid., p. 275.

[5]Edward M. Panosian, "Roman Catholicism: A Philosophy," *Focus on Missions,* Spring 1992, p. [3].

[6]Alister McGrath, *Evangelicalism and the Future of Christianity* (Downers Grove, Ill.: InterVarsity Press, 1995), p. 176.

[7]"Catholic Principles on Ecumenism," in *The Documents of Vatican II,* ed. Walter M. Abbott (New York: Guild Press, 1966), pp. 343-66.

[8]A good, brief overview of the history, teaching, and significance of Vatican II is H. M. Carson, "Vatican II," in *The New International Dictionary of the Christian Church,* ed. J. D. Douglas (Grand Rapids: Zondervan, 1974), pp. 1012-14.

[9]*Catechism of the Catholic Church* (Washington, D.C.: United States Catholic Conference, 1994). References to this catechism in the text are to paragraph numbers, not page numbers.

[10]McGrath, p. 172.

[11]A sympathetic introduction to Promise Keepers is Ken Abraham, *Who Are the Promise Keepers? Understanding the Christian Men's Movement* (New York: Doubleday, 1997). A balanced critique of the movement from a Reformed

perspective is found in David Hagopian and Douglas Wilson, *Beyond Promises: A Biblical Challenge to Promise Keepers* (Moscow, Idaho: Canon Press, 1996). Separatist objections to the movement are well summarized in Douglas R. McLachlan, "Promise Keepers: What's Really at Stake?" *Central Testimony,* Summer 1995, pp. 1-2, 5.

[12]Mike Aquilina, "Making New Catholic Men?" *Our Sunday Visitor,* 20 July 1997, pp. 10-11.

[13]The text of ECT was published in Neuhaus's periodical: "Evangelicals and Catholics Together: The Christian Mission in the Third Millennium," *First Things,* May 1994, pp. 15-22; all references to ECT are from this version. The controversy over ECT is summarized in Geisler and MacKenzie, pp. 491-502.

[14]"Evangelicals and Catholics Together," p. 21.

[15]Ibid., pp. 17-18.

[16]Ibid., p. 16.

[17]The important differences between the Catholic and Protestant views of justification, and the ramifications of those differences, are thoroughly discussed in R. C. Sproul, *Faith Alone: The Evangelical Doctrine of Justification* (Grand Rapids: Baker, 1995). Stung by criticisms such as Sproul's, many of the Roman Catholics and Evangelicals involved in ECT met in New York on October 7, 1997, to issue a second document, "The Gift of Salvation," published in *Christianity Today,* 8 December 1997, pp. 35-38. The statement makes declarations such as the following: "We agree that justification is not earned by any good works or merits of our own"; "In justification, God, on the basis of Christ's righteousness alone, declares us to be no longer his rebellious enemies but his forgiven friends"; "The New Testament makes it clear that the gift of justification is received through faith alone." Finally it concludes, "We understand that what we here affirm is in agreement with what the Reformation traditions have meant by justification by faith alone" (p. 36). However, the document says that one of the questions still to be discussed is "the historic uses of the language of justification as it relates to imputed or transformative righteousness" (p. 38). In other words, it admits that there is yet a gap between the biblical Protestant idea that in justification God declares the sinner righteous on the basis of Christ's righteousness and the Catholic teaching that in justification (which includes sanctification) a person becomes more righteous himself. Also, the document, like the original ECT, views Evangelical Christianity and Catholicism as equally valid expressions of Christianity. Furthermore, even if a group of Catholics such as those involved in ECT should be able to accede to a biblical definition of justification, their agreement would not change the official Catholic teaching as expressed in the Canons and Decrees of the Council of Trent, *Catechism of the Catholic Church,* and other official Catholic documents.

[18]J. Gresham Machen, *Christianity and Liberalism* (1923; reprint, Grand Rapids: Eerdmans, 1981), p. 52.

[19]Panosian, p. [2].

[20]Sproul, pp. 175-92.

[21]McGrath, p. 178. He discusses the idea of Catholic-Evangelical relations on pp. 175-80.

[22]Panosian, p. [3].

Glossary of Terms

apostasy: In its biblical sense, apostasy is the repudiation of the Christian faith by persons or organizations, even though they may maintain the name "Christian." The term *apostate* is sometimes applied to an individual who himself has not personally repudiated Christian truth but who belongs to groups characterized by apostasy and holds to teachings characteristic of apostasy.

cessationist: One who believes that special spiritual gifts such as speaking in tongues ceased with the close of the New Testament era.

Charismatic movement, the: Also known as Neo-Pentecostalism, the Charismatic movement is a variant of Pentecostalism (q.v.). Emerging in the 1960s, the movement is similar to Pentecostalism in stressing the exercise of spiritual gifts, notably speaking in tongues. The differences with Pentecostalism are that Charismatics remain members in major denominations and hold to looser standards of personal and ecclesiastical separation.

discipline in the church: Church discipline is action taken by the body of believers to correct the disobedience of one of its members. The goal of such discipline is to preserve the purity of the church and to reclaim the disobedient Christian.

disobedient brother: A professing Christian who, despite admonition, deliberately refuses to modify some aspect of his conduct or belief to conform to the clear teaching of Scripture is a disobedient brother.

dispensationalism: Dispensationalism is a system of biblical interpretation named for the different ages, or *dispensations,* seen in history. In each of these dispensations, God tests mankind in some way, and each age ends with man's failure and God's judgment. Central to dispensationalism is a distinction between Israel and the church. Certain parts of the Bible, including a great deal of prophecy, apply only to the Jews, and other parts apply only to Christians. Among the distinctive dispensationalist teachings is the Rapture (q.v.).

ecclesiastical separation: Ecclesiastical separation is in many ways the application of the principles of personal separation (q.v.) practiced on the level of an assembly of believers. It involves a refusal to align with false doctrine or unbelief and a rejection of the willful practice of disobedience. Discipline in the church (q.v.) is a form of ecclesiastical separation.

ecumenical movement: The word *ecumenical* means "universal" or "worldwide." The ecumenical movement refers to the attempt to unite all Christian churches, usually on a liberal basis that downplays important doctrinal matters.

Evangelical: During the Reformation the term *Evangelical* was virtually synonymous with "Protestant." As a result of the awakenings of the 1700s, the term *Evangelical* came to refer to Protestants who stress teachings such as the authority of Scripture alone, the substitutionary atonement of Christ, the new birth, the importance of holy living, and evangelism. Today, the term is used mainly for "any non-Fundamentalist conservative who does not accept or practice the principle of ecclesiastical separation" (David Beale). *See also* New Evangelicalism.

Evangelical cobelligerence: An idea credited to Reformed apologist Francis Schaeffer, the concept of Evangelical cobelligerence states that Evangelicals may work in temporary alliances with religious groups with whom they disagree as long as they share a common goal, such as a particular political or moral reform.

exclusivism: Exclusivism is the belief that a religious body such as a church or denomination should exclude all religious teaching contrary to the doctrinal standards of the church or denomination. In the Fundamentalist-Modernist Controversy, for example, the Fundamentalists were the exclusivist party. *See also* inclusivism.

existentialism: Existentialism is the philosophy that maintains that every person must face the inescapable fact that existence is the basic truth of life. Meaning in life comes not from some authority but from a person's own decisions and actions. Life itself has no purpose or meaning, so the individual must create his own meaning by his actions. At its most extreme, existentialism holds that truth is completely subjective. Because there is often no rational basis for committing to a certain course of action, an individual must make a "leap of faith" and commit himself to such a course apart from or even in spite of rational considerations.

false teacher: Someone who professes to be a Christian but who attempts to deceive the church by false doctrine is a false teacher.

Regardless of his personal standing with God, such a person teaches doctrine that threatens the eternal well-being of souls.

first-degree separation: Used by some Christians in reference to ecclesiastical separation, first-degree separation refers to refusing to cooperate with false teachers in religious activities; it is also known as primary separation. *See also* second-degree separation.

fundamental doctrine: A fundamental doctrine is a clear scriptural teaching that the Bible itself indicates is an important truth of Christianity. It is a teaching so essential to Christianity that it cannot be denied without destroying Christianity. Among the fundamental doctrines are the inspiration and authority of the Bible, the virgin birth of Christ, His deity, His absolute sinlessness, His substitutionary death on the cross, His bodily resurrection, His personal return, and the reality of heaven and hell.

Fundamentalism: Fundamentalism is a militant form of orthodox Protestantism arising in the United States in the late nineteenth and early twentieth centuries. Its central belief is that there are certain truths so essential to Christianity that they cannot be denied without destroying Christianity and that these essentials are the basis of Christian fellowship.

heresy: The word *heresy* is normally used to describe a dangerously false teaching, but the biblical use of the word often has the meaning of "division" (I Cor. 11:19; Gal. 5:20). *Heresy* came to mean "false doctrine" probably because false teachings create divisions.

higher criticism: Higher criticism is the study of the content of the Bible, dealing with questions of the authorship, date, and literary structure of the books of the Bible. The term is often viewed with suspicion by conservative Christians because liberal higher critics with faulty assumptions about the Bible's nature undermine the Scripture's authority by their conclusions. Reverent scholars with a high view of the Bible's inspiration, however, can also practice higher criticism. *See also* lower criticism.

holiness: In the biblical sense of the word, holiness is essentially uniqueness or "differentness." The difference is fundamentally moral (e.g., difference between good and evil or between God and Satan). The Bible expresses this uniqueness as moral purity and separation from that which is unclean. It is not primarily an external attribute but an internal one expressing itself externally.

inclusivism: Inclusivism is the belief that a religious body such as a church or denomination should include a wide range of theological beliefs, despite how those beliefs may clash with the traditional standards of belief for that body or church. In the Fundamentalist-Modernist Controversy, for example, the Modernists were the inclusivist party. *See also* exclusivism.

Keswick holiness: A system of teaching named for a conference site in England, the Keswick approach stresses the need for personal holiness through the power of the Holy Spirit. Among its distinctive ideas are the "victorious" or "abundant" life, the existence of two distinct natures in the believer (a corrupt old nature and a regenerate new nature), and a special experience following conversion (often called "surrender") in which a Christian moves to a higher level of spiritual development and maturity.

legalism: Theologically, legalism is the heresy of trying to earn merit with God by performing good works. As commonly used, however, legalism is requiring Christians to follow standards of behavior that have no basis in the Bible.

liberalism, religious: Broadly speaking, religious liberalism is an approach to the Christian faith based on the presuppositions of the Enlightenment. It assumes that reason and science are sure roads to truth and that human reason or experience is the test of the validity of religious ideas.

love: Defined biblically, love is a disposition to act in the highest interests of the loved one, regardless of the cost to the one who loves. Such a disposition may or may not involve an emotional attachment to the loved object, but it will unquestionably involve a self-sacrificial commitment.

lower criticism: Also called textual criticism, lower criticism is the study of the surviving manuscripts of the Bible. Textual critics endeavor to determine the exact reading of the original Scripture by a careful study of all available manuscripts. *See also* higher criticism.

Modernism: Modernism is the name for a form of religious liberalism (q.v.) influential in the United States in the late nineteenth and early twentieth centuries.

Neo-Fundamentalism: Arising in the 1970s, Neo-Fundamentalism was a movement that sought to reform Fundamentalism by modifying Fundamentalism's practice of separation and by involving conservative Christians in right-wing political causes. It differed initially from the New Evangelicalism (q.v.) in its reluctance to build bridges to theological liberals.

Neo-Liberalism: A post-1920s revision of Modernism in the United States, Neo-Liberalism stresses greater realism and less optimism concerning the nature of humanity and progress in world affairs.

Neo-orthodoxy: Neo-orthodoxy arose after World War I as an attempt to correct the excesses of theological liberalism. It claims to restore such orthodox biblical ideas as the pervasiveness of sin, God's transcendence, and the need of redemption. Critics charge, however, that the Neo-orthodox redefines such terms in an unbiblical manner. Neo-orthodoxy is characterized by a subjective view of revelation; the Bible is not itself God's Word but is a channel of revelation as the Holy Spirit speaks to the individual. Neo-orthodoxy borrows from existentialism (q.v.) and is sometimes called "the theology of crisis" because commitment to truth is often viewed as a leap of faith resulting from an inner crisis.

Neo-Pentecostalism: *See* Charismatic movement.

New Evangelicalism, the: Specifically, *the New Evangelicalism* refers to a movement in conservative Protestantism in America that arose in the 1940s and 1950s. Among the emphases of the New Evangelicals were a stress on scholarship, an accommodation to evolutionary theory, and a repudiation of ecclesiastical separation as practiced by Fundamentalists. More generally, the term has been used to describe any non-Fundamentalist Evangelical. Fundamentalists are the only major group still using the term *the New Evangelicalism;* most observers use simply the term *Evangelical* (q.v.) as the general designation.

Pentecostalism: Arising in the United States in the early 1900s, Pentecostalism is a form of Protestant Christianity that holds to the restoration of New Testament spiritual gifts. The most notable of these gifts is speaking in tongues as a sign of the baptism of the Holy Spirit. *See also* the Charismatic movement.

personal separation: Basically, personal separation is the practice of individual sanctification in refusing to follow the world's philosophy in thought and action.

positional sanctification: *See* sanctification.

postmillennialism: Postmillennialism is the belief that the Holy Spirit will work through the church until the gospel spreads throughout the world. When the world has been brought to Christ, then Jesus Himself will return for the final judgment. *See also* premillennialism *and* Rapture.

postmodernism: Postmodernism is a philosophical system arising in the latter half of the twentieth century that denies the rationalist basis of the Enlightenment. Postmodernists argue that human reason does not lead to a single unified view of reality and that scientific study is not a sure means to truth. Postmodernism makes truth a matter of individual perception. ("There are no facts, only interpretations.")

premillennialism: Premillennialism is the belief that there will be a great outpouring of God's wrath upon the earth followed by Christ's return to establish a millennial (thousand-year) kingdom. *See also* postmillennialism.

progressive sanctification: *See* sanctification.

Rapture: Based on the idea that Christ's return comes in two stages, the Rapture is the coming of Christ for His people just before God's wrath is poured out on earth. This teaching is commonly, but not exclusively, associated with dispensationalism.

realistic theology: Realistic theology is the name given to the form of Neo-orthodoxy (q.v.) advocated by Reinhold and H. Richard Niebuhr.

sanctification: Sanctification is the "setting apart" of a Christian unto God when he is converted. Positional sanctification is the Christian's status "in Christ" in which the holiness of Christ is credited to the Christian so that God views him as holy. Progressive sanctification is the process of realizing positional sanctification through personal growth in faith and holiness of life.

schism: D. Martyn Lloyd-Jones defines schism as "division in the true visible church about matters that are not sufficient to justify division or separation."

second-degree separation: Used by some Christians in reference to ecclesiastical separation, second-degree separation is refusing to have fellowship with someone who does not practice first-degree separation (separation from false teaching); it is also known as secondary separation. Many separatists do not recognize a distinction between first- and second-degree separation. *See also* first-degree separation.

separation: Essentially, biblical separation is the realization of progressive sanctification in a believer's life by striving to be free of the presence of sin. The term may also be used in connection with a church body's growth in purity (cf. I Cor. 5:7-8).

"signs and wonders" movement: *See* third wave.

social gospel: The social gospel is the teaching pioneered by Walter Rauschenbusch (1861-1918) that the gospel needs to be applied to social institutions. The social gospel downplays original sin and Christ's atonement to stress individual personal reform and bringing all social organizations under the law of Christ. The goal of the social gospel is to build the kingdom of God on earth by human effort. The phrase "social gospel" is generally used by conservatives to mean a system of social reform with little reference to individual redemption through the atonement of Jesus Christ.

soteriology: Soteriology is the study of the doctrines concerning salvation.

theology of crisis: *See* Neo-orthodoxy.

third wave: Also known as the "signs and wonders" movement, the third wave is an outgrowth of the Pentecostal and Charismatic movements dating from the 1980s. It supposedly follows Pentecostalism and the Charismatic movement as the third wave of the Holy Spirit's blessing. Its adherents claim to be neither Pentecostal nor Charismatic but seek the same kind of spiritual gifts. Supporters of this position claim that miraculous signs and wonders (healings, exorcisms, etc.) are necessary to proclaim the gospel.

tradition: Sometimes called oral tradition, "tradition" in Roman Catholic teaching refers to a body of oral teaching that Christ gave to the apostles along with the written Scriptures. Catholics consider this tradition of equal authority with the Bible. Catholics recognize the church, under the leadership of the pope and the bishops, as the authoritative interpreter of tradition. Tradition is allegedly expressed in the interpretations of the church fathers (ancient), church doctors (medieval), and popes.

Trent, Council of: Held in three sessions from 1545 to 1563, the Council of Trent was the official Catholic response to the Protestant Reformation. The council specifically condemned Protestant teachings and demanded submission to the official teaching of the Catholic Church as newly defined by the church hierarchy.

Vatican II: More properly called the Second Vatican Council, this Roman Catholic assembly met from 1962 to 1965. The council enacted many reforms, such as replacing Latin in its services with the vernacular. It also adopted a much friendlier tone toward non-Catholics.

The council did not, however, significantly narrow the gap between Catholic teaching and historic Protestant teaching.

worldliness: Worldliness is an attitude of friendship toward, a desire for, and a wish to be recognized by the world system. It is sometimes used of the behavior of people characterized by this inner attitude.

world system: In contrast to the physical world, the world system refers to the unregenerate people of this earth as organized and dominated by Satan.

Select Bibliography

Books and Pamphlets

Ashbrook, John. *Axioms of Separation.* Mentor, Ohio: Here I Stand Books, n.d.

———. *The New Neutralism II.* Mentor, Ohio: Here I Stand Books, 1992.

Beale, David O. *In Pursuit of Purity: American Fundamentalism Since 1850.* Greenville, S.C.: Unusual Publications, 1986.

Budgen, Victor. *The Charismatics and the Word of God.* Welwyn, England: Evangelical Press, 1985.

Burgess, Stanley M., and Gary B. McGee, ed., *Dictionary of the Pentecostal and Charismatic Movements.* Grand Rapids: Zondervan Publishing House, Regency Reference Library, 1988.

Cairns, Alan. *Apostles of Error.* Greenville, S.C.: Faith Presbyterian Church, 1989.

Carnell, Edward John. *The Case for Orthodox Theology.* Philadelphia: Westminster Press, 1959.

Carpenter, Joel. *Revive Us Again: The Reawakening of American Fundamentalism.* New York: Oxford University Press, 1997.

Cohen, Gary G. *Biblical Separation Defended: A Biblical Critique of Ten New Evangelical Arguments.* Philadelphia: Presbyterian and Reformed, 1966.

Dollar, George. *A History of Fundamentalism in America.* Greenville, S.C.: Bob Jones University Press, 1973.

Erickson, Millard. *The Evangelical Left: Encountering Postconservative Evangelical Theology.* Grand Rapids: Baker, 1997.

———. *The New Evangelical Theology.* Westwood, N.J.: Revell, 1968.

Falwell, Jerry, Ed Dobson, and Ed Hindson. *The Fundamentalist Phenomenon: The Resurgence of Conservative Christianity.* Garden City, N.Y.: Doubleday-Galilee, 1981.

Ferm, Robert O. *Cooperative Evangelism: Is Billy Graham Right or Wrong?* Grand Rapids: Zondervan, 1958.

Geisler, Norman L., and Ralph E. MacKenzie. *Roman Catholics and Evangelicals: Agreements and Disagreements.* Grand Rapids: Baker, 1995.

Gundry, Stanley N., and Alan F. Johnson, ed. *Tensions in Contemporary Theology.* Chicago: Moody, 1976.

Henry, Carl F. H. *The Uneasy Conscience of Modern Fundamentalism.* Grand Rapids: Eerdmans, 1947.

Hordern, William. *The Case for a New Reformation Theology.* Philadelphia: Westminster Press, 1959.

———. *A Layman's Guide to Protestant Theology.* Rev. ed. New York: Macmillan, 1968.

Hunter, James Davison. *Evangelicalism: The Coming Generation.* Chicago: University of Chicago Press, 1987.

Jones, Bob. *Scriptural Separation: "First and Second Degree."* Greenville, S.C.: Bob Jones University Press, 1971.

Lindsell, Harold. *The Battle for the Bible.* Grand Rapids: Zondervan, 1976.

Lloyd-Jones, D. Martyn. *Knowing the Times: Addresses Delivered on Various Occasions 1942-1977.* Edinburgh: Banner of Truth, 1989.

MacArthur, John. *Charismatic Chaos.* Grand Rapids: Zondervan, 1992.

Machen, J. Gresham. *Christianity and Liberalism.* 1923. Reprint, Grand Rapids: Eerdmans, 1981.

Marsden, George. *Fundamentalism and American Culture: The Shaping of Twentieth-Century Evangelicalism, 1870-1925.* New York: Oxford University Press, 1980.

————. *Reforming Fundamentalism: Fuller Seminary and the New Evangelicalism.* Grand Rapids: Eerdmans, 1987.

————. *Understanding Fundamentalism and Evangelicalism.* Grand Rapids: Eerdmans, 1991.

Martin, William C. *Prophet with Honor: The Billy Graham Story.* New York: Morrow, 1991.

Marty, Martin E. *Modern American Religion.* 3 vols. Chicago: University of Chicago Press, 1986, 1991, 1996.

Masters, Peter. *Stand for the Truth.* London: Sword and Trowel, 1996.

McCarthy, James G. *The Gospel According to Rome: Comparing Catholic Tradition and the Word of God.* Eugene, Ore.: Harvest House, 1995.

McCune, Rolland D. *Ecclesiastical Separation.* Allen Park, Mich.: Detroit Baptist Theological Seminary, n.d.

McGrath, Alister. *Evangelicalism and the Future of Christianity.* Downers Grove, Ill.: InterVarsity Press, 1995.

McLachlan, Douglas R. *Reclaiming Authentic Fundamentalism.* Independence, Mo.: American Association of Christian Schools, 1993.

Moore, Howard Edgar. "The Emergence of Moderate Fundamentalism: John R. Rice and 'The Sword of the Lord.' " Ph.D. diss., George Washington University, 1990.

Moritz, Fred. *"Be Ye Holy": The Call to Christian Separation.* Greenville, S.C.: Bob Jones University Press, 1994.

Nash, Ronald. *The New Evangelicalism.* Grand Rapids: Zondervan, 1963.

Pickering, Ernest D. *The Biblical Doctrine of Separation.* Clarks Summit, Pa.: Baptist Bible College, 1976.

————. *Biblical Separation: The Struggle for a Pure Church.* Schaumburg, Ill.: Regular Baptist Press, 1979.

———. *Charismatic Confusion.* Schaumburg, Ill.: Regular Baptist Press, 1980.

———. *The Tragedy of Compromise: The Origin and Impact of the New Evangelicalism.* Greenville, S.C.: Bob Jones University Press, 1994.

Reymond, Robert L. *Introductory Studies in Contemporary Theology.* Philadelphia: Presbyterian and Reformed, 1968.

Quebedeaux, Richard. *The Worldly Evangelicals.* New York: Harper and Row, 1978.

———. *The Young Evangelicals: Revolution in Orthodoxy.* New York: Harper and Row, 1974.

Rice, John R. *Come Out or Stay In.* Nashville: Thomas Nelson, 1974.

———. *Earnestly Contending for the Faith.* Murfreesboro, Tenn.: Sword of the Lord, 1965.

Ryrie, Charles Caldwell. *Neo-Orthodoxy.* Chicago: Moody Press, 1956.

Sandeen, Ernest. *The Roots of Fundamentalism: British and American Millenarianism, 1800-1930.* 1970. Reprint, Grand Rapids: Baker, 1978.

Schaff, David. *Our Fathers Faith and Ours: A Comparison Between Protestantism and Romanism.* 2nd ed. New York: G. P. Putnam's Sons, 1928.

Smith, David L. *A Handbook of Contemporary Theology.* Wheaton, Ill.: BridgePoint, 1992.

Spence, O. Talmadge. *Charismatism, Awakening or Apostasy?* Greenville, S.C.: Bob Jones University Press, 1978.

———. *Pentecostalism: Purity or Peril?* Greenville, S.C.: Unusual Publications, 1989.

Sproul, R. C. *Faith Alone: The Evangelical Doctrine of Justification.* Grand Rapids: Baker, 1995.

Torrey, R. A., A. C. Dixon, et al. *The Fundamentals: A Testimony to the Truth.* 4 vols. 1917. Reprint, Grand Rapids: Baker, 1988.

Tulga, Chester. *The Doctrine of Separation in These Times.* Chicago: Conservative Baptist Fellowship, 1952.

Van Til, Cornelius. *The New Modernism: An Appraisal of the Theology of Barth and Brunner.* 3rd ed. N.p.: Presbyterian and Reformed, 1973.

Wesley, John. *A Plain Account of Christian Perfection.* Louisville: Pentecostal Publishing, n.d.

Woodbridge, Charles. *Bible Separation.* Halifax: The Peoples Gospel Hour Press, 1971.

Woodbridge, John D. *Biblical Authority.* Grand Rapids: Zondervan, 1982.

Articles

Barnhouse, Donald Grey. "One Church." *Eternity,* July 1958, pp. 17-23.

———. "Thanksgiving and Warning." *Eternity,* September 1957, pp. 9, 44-45.

Bell, L. Nelson. "On 'Separation.' " *Christianity Today,* 8 October 1971, pp. 26-27.

Eenigenburg, Elton M. "Separatism Is Not Scriptural." *Eternity,* August 1963, pp. 16, 18-22.

Fea, John. "Understanding the Changing Facade of Twentieth-Century American Protestant Fundamentalism: Toward a Historical Definition." *Trinity Journal* 15 (1994): 181-99.

Graham, Billy. "The Lost Chord of Evangelism." *Christianity Today,* 1 April 1957, p. 26.

Grounds, Vernon. "Separation Yes, Schism No." *Eternity,* August 1963, pp. 17-22.

Horton, Robert Lon. "The Christian's Role in Society." *Biblical Viewpoint* 15 (1981): 130-37.

Huffman, Jerry. "Separation—The Big 'S' Word." *Frontline,* January-February 1992, p. 5.

"Is Evangelical Theology Changing?" *Christian Life,* March 1956, pp. 16-19.

Jones, Bob. "Pseudo-fundamentalists: The New Breed in Sheep's Clothing," *Faith for the Family,* January 1978, pp. 7, 16.

Jones III, Bob. "The Moral Majority." *Faith for the Family,* September 1980, pp. 3, 27-28.

———. "The Ultimate Ecumenism." *Faith for the Family,* September 1985, pp. 3, 9-10.

Leedy, Randy. "The Ethic of Love." *Biblical Viewpoint* 30, no. 1 (1996): 5-14.

Lightner, Robert. "A Biblical Perspective on False Doctrine." *Bibliotheca Sacra* 142 (1985): 16-22.

Martin, Walter R. "Love, Doctrine, and Fellowship: How Can We Put Them Together?" *Eternity,* November 1960, pp. 20-22, 56-57.

———. "When Is Separation Necessary?" *Eternity,* January 1961, pp. 30-31.

McCune, Rolland D. "The Self-Identity of Fundamentalism." *Detroit Baptist Theological Seminary Journal* 1 (1996): 9-34.

———. "Separation: An Important Benchmark of True Fundamentalism." *Frontline,* May-June 1993, pp. 15-17.

McIntire, C. T. "Fundamentalism." In *Evangelical Dictionary of Theology.* Ed. Walter Elwell. Grand Rapids: Baker, 1984, pp. 433-36.

Nutz, Earl. "Important Lessons: I John 2." *Biblical Viewpoint* 27, no. 1 (1993): 31-37.

Pulliam, Ken R. "Christian Standards Are Not Legalism." *Frontline,* September-October 1991, p. 7.

Runia, Klaas. "When Is Separation a Christian Duty?" *Christianity Today,* 23 June 1967, pp. 3-5; 7 July 1967, pp. 6-8.

Sanderson, John W. "Fundamentalism and Its Critics." *Sunday School Times,* 21 January 1961, pp. 58-59, 66.

————. "Fundamentalism and Neo-Evangelicalism—Whither?" *Sunday School Times,* 4 February 1961, pp. 90-91, 101-2.

————. "Neo-Evangelicalism and Its Critics." *Sunday School Times,* 28 January 1961, pp. 74, 82.

————. "Purity of Testimony—or Opportunity?" *Sunday School Times,* 11 February 1961, pp. 110-11.

Sweeney, Douglas. "Fundamentalism and the Neo-Evangelicals." *Fides et Historia* 24, no. 1 (1992): 81-96.

Woodbridge, John D. "Is Biblical Inerrancy a Fundamentalist Doctrine?" *Bibliotheca Sacra* 142 (1985): 292-305.

————. "A Neoorthodox Historiography Under Siege." *Bibliotheca Sacra* 142 (1985): 3-15.

————. "The Rogers and McKim Proposal in the Balance." *Bibliotheca Sacra* 142 (1985): 99-113.

Scripture Index

Subject Index

Rauschenbusch, Walter, 97, 181
Reagan, Ronald, 124
realistic theology, 107, 180
Reformation, 73, 91, 113, 142, 176, 181
Rice, John R., 20, 61, 81, 83, 124
Riley, W. B., 78, 79, 134
Ritschl, Albrecht, 95
Roberts, Oral, 131-32, 136-37, 173 n. 21
Robertson, Pat, 133, 149
Rogers, Jack, 111
Roman Catholicism, 9, 70, 86, 99, 100, 125-26, 132, 138, 141-54, 174 n. 17, 181
Rudnick, Milton, 88
Runia, Klaas, 32, 51, 157 n. 18, 159 n. 16
Rushdoony, Rousas, 9
Ryrie, Charles, 107, 109

sacraments (Catholic), 144, 147
sanctification, 2-3, 144, 180
Sanderson, John, 127
Schaeffer, Francis, 126, 147, 176
schism, 14-15, 26, 63, 180
Scofield, C. I., 77
Scofield Reference Bible, 77
Scopes Trial, 80, 116
Second Vatican Council.
  See Vatican II
separation, v-vi, 26, 117, 120-23, 153, 180-81
  church and state, 6, 10
  ecclesiastical, 4-5, 8-10, 41, 55-56, 137-38, 175-76, 180
  first-degree, 5-6, 66, 124-25, 176
  from disobedient Christians, 55-68, 70, 127, 151, 153
  from false teachers, 41-53, 70, 101, 111, 150, 151, 153
  from the world, 27-40, 153
  personal, 4, 7-8, 41, 55, 137, 179
  primary. *See* separation, first-degree

secondary. *See* separation, second-degree
  second-degree, 5-6, 66, 124-25, 180
"separated brethren," 146
700 Club, The, 133
Seymour, William J., 130, 131
Shakarian, Demos, 132
Shakers, 130
"Shall the Fundamentalists Win?" 97, 101
"Shall Unbelief Win?" 101
Shields, T. T., 79
"shunning," 64
"signs and wonders" movement. *See* third wave
Smith, Wilbur, 167 n. 6
social gospel, 97, 116, 181
social involvement of Christians, 116-17. *See also* Evangelical cobelligerence
soteriology, 2, 181
Sproul, R. C., 126, 150, 174 n. 17
Spurgeon, Charles H., 10, 87
Stendahl, Krister, 138, 172-73 n. 21
Sumner, Robert L., 85
Sunday, Billy, 74
Sunday School Times, 81
Swaggart, Jimmy, 137
Sword of the Lord, 1, 83, 124

Taylor, Hudson, 71
Tertullian, 7
textual criticism. *See* lower criticism
theology of crisis, 104, 179
third wave, 133-34, 181
Tillich, Paul, 108
Toronto blessing, 134
tradition (Catholic teaching), 143, 150, 181
Trent, Council of, 142, 147, 174 n. 17, 181
Trinity, 12, 71
Tulga, Chester, 32